CONTENTS

INTRODUCTION:
ONE MAN'S VISION

At the dawn of the twenty-first century, Christianity had approximately 2.2 billion adherents, with Roman Catholics alone numbering more than 1.1 billion. It has established itself as the predominant religion in Europe, the Americas, Oceania, Russia, and large parts of sub-Saharan Africa. The Bible is said to be the most printed book in the world and the number-one bestseller of all time. As the faith of perhaps a third of the world's population, it is the most successful of the world religions if numbers are used as the criteria. How did this happen? And what is the secret to its success?

On October 28, 312, two opposing armies met near a stone bridge over the River Tiber just north of Rome. The ensuing battle would be recorded in history as the Battle of Milvian Bridge. This struggle between rival generals for succession to the throne of the Roman Empire was triggered when the reign of Diocletian came to an end on May 1, 305. In Rome, Marcus Aurelius Valerius Maxentius had assumed the title of emperor, whereas Flavius Valerius Aurelius Constantinus was proclaimed Augustus in a fortified city in Roman-occupied Britain known today as York. Constantinus is better known in history as Constantine the Great. A showdown was inevitable. By the spring of 312, Constantine's forces had made inroads into northern Italy and won major battles against the supporters of Maxentius. Finally, Maxentius met Constantine as the latter's army marched toward the imperial capital. The battle that took place was just like any other battle. There was a victor and a vanquished. Constantine's forces

E Ong

broke the lines formed by Maxentius's soldiers and drove them into the Tiber. Maxentius's mistake of organizing his troops into long lines with their backs facing the river made retreat almost impossible. Many who fled were drowned, including Maxentius himself, who was inadvertently pushed into the water by his fleeing troops.

Fighting between commanders of Roman legions for the throne has been a recurring theme. So what made this event significant? It was not because Maxentius and Constantine were brothers-in-law nor the fact that Maxentius had a larger force. Nothing about the battle was remarkable or unusual.

The accession of Constantine following his victory at the Battle of Milvian Bridge laid the foundation for Christianity to eventually become the dominant faith. Jesus said, "He who live by the sword shall perish by the sword." Ironically, it was as a result of a victory won by the sword that the religion of Christ prevailed. In 313, the Edict of Milan was issued, granting Christians freedom to practice their creed. Until then, Christians were severely persecuted, and many were martyred for their beliefs. The crosses put up in the Colosseum are in memory of the many Christians whose lives came to a horrific end in the empire's largest amphitheater. Suddenly, Roman lions lost their staple food, and its captive population began to quickly dwindle. For his role in promulgating Christianity, Constantine is canonized as a saint in the Eastern Orthodox Church. Yet even in modern times, historians continue to debate about the circumstances of his conversion.

A number of modern-day evangelical preachers have proclaimed that after many decades of tribulation when Christians have shown their devotion to their savior by tenaciously clinging on to their faith, God finally delivered them by reducing the pagan Romans to submission. Constantine was God's instrument to bring about this divine transformation. But why did God choose an unbeliever? What is even more surprising was that Constantine remained in many ways a pagan throughout his reign. It is doubtful that he experienced what evangelical Christians in this day and age would describe as a born-again experience. After his accession to the throne, there was no drastic change in the religious landscape of the Roman Empire. Most of the influential people in Constantine's government remained pagan. None of the monuments he immediately commissioned as emperor, including the Arch of Constantine, made any reference to Christianity. On the contrary, the arch celebrating his victory at Milvian Bridge was inscribed with the images of Victoria and Roman deities such as Apollo, Diana, and Hercules. The sun god Apollo remained a favorite of Constantine.

In 321, Constantine urged his subjects, both Christians and pagans, to observe the "venerable day of the sun." Years into his reign, Roman coins still bore the images of pagan gods and symbols of the sun cult. In 330, Constantinople, his new capital and eventual seat of Byzantine Christianity, was consecrated. Even on this occasion, he wore an ornamental headband with symbols of Apollo. The goddess Tyche was shown placed in the hand of the emperor's statue on the Column of Constantine. The city's pagan temples, including shrines to Dioscuri and Tyche, flourished. Although the emperor continued to engage in pagan rituals, he became more Christian over the years. Finally, toward the end of his life, Constantine formally converted and accepted baptism. He, however, retained the title Pontifex Maximus, the head of the pagan priesthood traditionally borne by emperors, until his demise. This title would later be applied to the pope as the chief bishop of the Roman Catholic Church.

There was no stopping what Constantine set in motion. Christianity continued to grow from strength to strength in the Roman Empire under his successors. By the time Flavius Claudius Julianus became emperor in 355, Christianity was so entrenched that this last non-Christian ruler of the Roman Empire failed to revive pagan practices and purge Christian beliefs. Finally, in 391, Theodosius I made Christianity the state religion, paving the way for the proscription of paganism.

What prompted Constantine's conversion? Legend has it that when both armies were preparing for battle on the evening of October 27, Constantine received a heavenly vision. What he supposedly saw varied from source to source. The most popular version was that Constantine was commanded in a dream to mark a heavenly sign on the shields of his troops. That sign was Chi-Ro, the first two letters of the Greek spelling for "Christ" and commonly used to denote the messiah of the Christians. In another account, while he and his troops were marching, Constantine saw a cross of light above the sun with the Greek words: "In this sign, you shall conquer." Whatever transpired on the day of the battle, Constantine's soldiers took the field with unfamiliar symbols on their shields and standards. Many of the soldiers and their adversaries must have made little sense of them. This was no crusade or jihad. There were no reports of miracles or unexplained supernatural manifestations taking place as the two armies of non-Christians slaughtered each other. Nevertheless,

Constantine proclaimed that he believed his success was attributed to the favor of the High God of the Christians.

It was the Roman Empire that formed the nucleus for the spread of Christianity, resulting in its dominant position in the world today. The Roman road system spanning more than 400,000 kilometers facilitated the movement of people and ideas. Latin and Greek, the lingua francas of the empire, made communication much easier. Between the fifth and seventh centuries, a host of barbarian tribes conquered and settled in various parts of the Roman Empire. They were soon assimilated to the culture and religion of the more sophisticated local inhabitants whom they subjugated. In the fifth century, the Franks, a Germanic tribe, established a huge kingdom within and outside the former territories of the Roman Empire. Clovis I, the first king to unite all Frankish tribes, converted to his wife's Catholicism upon marriage and was baptized in 496. The Frankish empire in turn became an important agent in spreading Christianity among the inhabitants of Western Europe. Germanic peoples converted by the Franks, such as the Saxons, became instrumental in Christianizing the Slavs in central Europe. After the schism, both the Roman Catholic and the Byzantine Churches sent forth their missionaries to compete for converts.

In the early eleventh century, Christianity spread from the Byzantine Empire to the Kievan Rus. Vladimir the Great accepted baptism to marry the sister of the Byzantine emperor. The direct consequence of his decision is that the Russians, Ukrainians, Belorussians, and many other peoples in the former Russian empire practice Orthodox Christianity today. In the 1500s and 1600s, the

Spaniards and the Portuguese conquerors brought their Catholic faith to the New World, introducing it to millions of Native Americans and African slaves transported across the Atlantic. The population increase in Europe in the 1700s and 1800s would send millions all over the globe to search for fresh opportunities. Many of their descendants in the Americas and Australasia continue to practice the faith of their forefathers. In the second half of the nineteenth century, the scramble by the British, French, Dutch, and German to establish colonies in Africa and Asia would escalate. Missionaries followed in their wake, sowing the seeds of Christianity as they established schools, hospitals, and orphanages.

We will never know what exactly Constantine saw or dreamt. Some scientists have attributed a solar halo called a "sun dog" as a possible explanation based on the description of his vision. In other words, it was nothing more than a meteorological phenomenon that results in bright spots of light in the sky, often on a luminous ring or halo on either side of the sun. Pachacuti, the man who transformed a small Andean kingdom into the mighty Inca Empire, also believed he had a similar vision of the sun from "the Creator of Heaven and Earth" on the eve of a decisive battle in 1438. He, too, believed that he had received divine help against his enemies. But with no followers of Jesus In the Americas at that time, Pachachuti had no exposure to Christianity. Consequently, he came to a different conclusion from that of Constantine, and he built Coricancha, or the Temple of the Sun, in Cusco for this divine help.

What if Constantine had interpreted his vision differently? And what if he had embraced another religion? At the time of Constantine, Christianity was only one of a host of sects, most of which were also

6

from the Middle East, vying for followers among the Romans. Initially, Christianity was considered merely another offshoot of Judaism. Monotheism obviously appealed to many, and in the first and second centuries after Christ, the Jewish population had ballooned rapidly with conversions. So successful was it in gaining proselytes that some historians have claimed that Jews constituted 25 percent of the population in the Eastern Mediterranean and 10 percent in the entire empire, totaling as many as eight million people. Some converts were prominent people such as Flavius Clemens, a former consul and close relative of the emperor. A strange sect called the Manicheans after its founder, Mani, had also spread at a phenomenal speed throughout the Roman Empire. Drawing its beliefs from a number of other religions, it was considered a heretical offshoot of both Christianity and Zoroastrianism. The Christian theologian St. Augustine of Hippo was a champion of Manichaeism for years prior to his conversion. It is believed that Manichaean centers of worship had been established in Rome when Constantine marched triumphantly into the city. Christians, Jews, and Manicheans all suffered persecution at various times in the Roman Empire, including during the reign of Diocletian, Constantine's predecessor.

At the time of Constantine, there were also a number of Middle Eastern sects that shared a great deal of similarities with Judaism and Christianity but adhered to beliefs that we would consider as bizarre and unconventional. Today they are collectively known as Gnostics, from the Greek word "gnosis" for "knowledge." There the Elchasiates, who believed that two gigantic angels had revealed to their founder, Elchasaios, that, every century, Christ would be reborn and each time of a virgin. Observing Jewish laws, the Elchasites venerate water as the source of life and passed on a mystic formula to be used in the event that anyone among them was bitten by a mad dog or a snake. Then there were the Marcionites, who believed that not only the God referred to in the Old Testament was different from that of the New Testament but also that they were archenemies. They regarded the heroes of the Old Testament as the bad guys while holding in high regard Cain, the Sodomites, Nebuchadnezzar, and the serpent of the Garden of Eden. Other groups include the Messalians, who believed that when demons are exorcised, they would exit from the nose as mucus or from the mouth as saliva, and the Carpocratians, who maintained that the believer must scrupulously ignore the distinction between good and evil. Resisting conversion to Christianity and Islam, the only Gnostics who survived into the twentieth century were the Mandaeans, who revered John the Baptist. Numbering no more than 100,000, they resided mainly in Iraq and Iran until their dispersion as a result of the unrest in the aftermath of the 2003 invasion of Iraq. The precarious existence today of the Mandaeans and other small and little-known ancient Middle Eastern religious groups such as the Samaritans, Zoroastrians, Yazidis, and Yarsan in a sea of Islam reminds us of what could have easily been the fate of Christianity.

Ultimately, Christianity came to be the established faith of Europe and many parts of the world that came under European influence. The chain of causation can be traced clearly to the Romans, who became followers of Jesus not through a series of Billy Graham-styled revival meetings but because of one man's vision. Born to a Roman military officer in a town in present-day Serbia, Constantine played a more decisive role than St. Peter, St. Paul, or any disciple of

Christ. With a little luck, he became emperor as a result of his nemesis's tactical error. William Dalrymple, in his book *From the Holy Mountain*, puts forward the hypothetical scenario, "What if the Manichees or Gnostics could have won the day, so that on Sundays we would now read the Gospel of Philip (which emphasizes Jesus's lustily red-blooded attachment to Mary Magdalene) and applaud the Serpent of the Garden of Eden. Churches would be dedicated not to 'heretics' like St. John Chrsyotom but rather Manichean godlings such as the Great Nous and the Primal Man, and Messalian mucus-exorcisms would take place every Sunday after evensong."

Is success as certain as divine will, or is it no more than the roll of a dice? If things that happen happened at random then wouldn't all that separates success from failure be a precariously thin line?

CHAPTER 1:
HEADSTART

How lucky one is to be a great sportsman.

At the 2008 Beijing Olympics, Michael Phelps made history when he won the most Olympic gold medals with a total of sixteen. He was only twenty-three. Phelps has previously bagged six gold and two bronze in the 2004 Athens Olympics. But it was in Beijing that he made his mark by winning eight gold medals and thus surpassing the legendary Mark Spitz's performance of seven at Munich. The native of Baltimore, Maryland, finally broke his fellow US swimmer's thirty-six-year-old record of the most gold medals won in a single Olympics. From August 10–17, 2008, Phelps smashed seven world records in the eight events in which he participated at the Beijing National Aquatics Center. Although he did not break the world record in the hundred-meter butterfly event, an Olympic record was still set.

Even before the Beijing Olympics, the son of a state trooper and a school principal already made it as a millionaire. According to *The Wall Street Journal*, Phelps was paid $3 to $5 million annually from the ten sponsorships he brought to Beijing, which included Visa, Hilton, AT&T, and the renowned swimsuit manufacturer Speedo. Peter Carlisle, his agent, told *The Wall Street Journal* that Phelps received on the average fifty proposals daily from advertisers even prior to Beijing. After his historic acquisition of eight gold medals, some referred to him as history's greatest swimmer and even the "greatest Olympian ever." Phelps graced the covers of magazines, with *Sports Illustrated* publishing a photo of him with all eight of his gold medals won at Beijing. Sponsors were queuing to get him on board, and Carlisle estimated that his newfound fame should have been able to fetch him $100 million "over the course of his lifetime" through television commercials and appearances at public events.

Michael Phelps is a great sportsman. And that makes him very fortunate. Swimming and many other sports, you see, is a level playing field. Now imagine you are a participant in a swimming competition marching toward the pool with your competitors. There is no substitute for hard work. Like all athletes who strive to be at the top of their field, you live a highly disciplined life. Your arduous training regime involves waking up early and swimming laps for four hours, clocking a mileage of as many as ten kilometers in a day. Hours more are spent at the gym. You have made sacrifices in all aspects of your life. Ultimately, the moment you have been preparing for has arrived, and it all comes down to this race, which will be over within a matter of seconds. Stepping onto the block, you calm your nerves. You mentally visualize exactly how you intend to swim and finish the race. You adjust your goggles and relax your tensed muscles.

The gun goes off, and the race begins. Picture the moment when the swimmers plunge into the pool. Everybody is equal. The rules ensure that the race is fair. All the competitors await the same signal. They can only plunge from the starting blocks at the same time and not a split second faster. Anyone plunging in too soon will be disqualified. Each swimmer can take comfort that the person in the next lane is swimming the same distance as him. Nothing less. You have done everything in your power to prepare for this competition.

The hours of dedicated training count. It does not matter what is the color of your skin, which country you are from, or who you went to school with. The name of the college awarding your degree or the fact that you do not have one is irrelevant. The fact that the guy swimming in the next lane has a dad who earns millions a year while yours struggles with two jobs just to put food on the table gives him no advantage over you. There is no discrimination in the pool.

You race down the length of the pool and feel the water rush past every part of your body. Fully focused on completing, you are oblivious to the deafening cheers of the crowd. Your own breathing and pounding heart drown out the splashes and kicks of the competitors beside you as you slice through the water. You touch the wall and look up at the clock. When the race ends, the gold medal goes to the fastest sportsman. You see the name of the winner appearing on the board. It is you. For just a brief moment, you are dazed and bewildered. But your disbelief quickly gives way to jubilation as you roar with elation and smash the water with your fist. You are exuberant because your hard work paid off. Standing on the highest block of the podium with your medal, you acknowledge the crowd's thunderous applause and cheers. You make your country proud as the national anthem of your country is played. Tears of joy stream down the faces of your loved ones, who are among your most ardent supporters. The feeling of being number one is fantastic. You deserve it because you are the best. And that is that. Period. You have proven that you are the fastest among the participants who competed in this event, and the outcome cannot be disputed. Nobody could have swum the race for you even if they wanted to. And this would be the case even if your father were the richest man on earth.

So why is Michael Phelps lucky? The answer is simple. A swimming competition is nothing like the real world. At the international and Olympic levels, the sport of swimming is governed by the Federation Internationale de Natation, which is better known by its acronym, FINA. Like many other sports governing bodies, FINA sets out rules to ensure that no competitor has an unfair advantage. For example, the use of performance-enhancing drugs is prohibited. These rules have resulted in many swimmers being banned and having their medals stripped for doping violations. FINA has reiterated "the main and core principle that swimming is a sport essentially based on the physical performance of the athlete." So it should come as no surprise that when seventeen world records fell in the December 2008 European Short Course Championships, FINA looked into the adequacy of its rules on swimsuits. The line of high-end swimsuits manufactured by Speedo known as LZR Racer Suit had become quickly popular with competitors. Apparently, the combined effects of the LZR, which uses a high-technology swimwear fabric composed of woven elastane-nylon and polyurethane, give the swimmer an edge by both compressing the body and trapping air for buoyancy. Protests that the LZR was nothing less than "technological doping" led FINA to ban all body-length swimsuits and prescribe the suits' thickness and buoyancy. To the average person who swims for leisure, it might be hard to understand what the fuss was about. But to those competing in international meets, a split second makes a whole world of difference.

Are not the notions of fairness, which the rules in the world of sports strive to achieve, in stark contrast with those of the real world? Is it not the case that there will always be some who have a competitive edge? Success comes easier for some than others. We are never governed by the same rules. Using swimming as a metaphor, we do not plunge in the pool at the exact same moment. Imagine if one of the guys in the other lane is entitled to plunge in earlier or swim a shorter distance. Would not the outcome be different?

On August 14, 2008, it looked like there was a real danger that Phelps would see his hopes of eight gold medals torpedoed at Beijing's Water Cube. The American swimming sensation was trailing behind Serbian Milorad Cavic in the hundred-meter butterfly event. After Phelps collected six gold medals in the previous events, it appeared that his winning streak was about to end. At some point in the final phase of the race, many believed that overtaking the relatively unknown Cavic was insurmountable. At fifty meters, Phelps was behind by 0.62 seconds, which, in swimming parlance, was a substantial margin. It was a nail-biting finish, and Phelps needed all of his six-foot-seven frame and massive hands to keep his dream alive. As he was participating in only eight events, he needed to win every race he was in. You could imagine the enormous pressure Phelps must have been facing. Even in the last strokes toward the wall, it appeared that the Serbian would emerge as the winner. Interestingly, prior to the hundred-meter butterfly finals, Cavic apparently created a stir when he said, "It would be nice if historians talk about Michael Phelps winning seven gold medals and losing the eighth to 'some guy.' I'd like to be that guy." There was a brief moment of uncertainty when the race ended, as both appeared to have touched simultaneously. Finally, the times flashed on the scoreboard were Phelps 50.58 and Cavic 50.59. Yes, so close. Almost immediately, the Serbians filed a protest, but FINA remained firm with their decision after watching a frame-by-frame replay of the finishing touches. It was the slimmest possible margin. This time, Phelps had luck on his side. Faster than a blink of an eye, one one-hundredth of a second, the smallest measurement in swimming, was all that separated Phelps from his nearest competitor. Who could say what the outcome would be if there was an immediate rematch and they swam again? One wonders how the FINA officials would determine if this race were completed decades ago before the advent of such state-of-the-art technology.

Only fractions of a second separate the swimming competitors who will receive the gold, silver, and bronze medals or none at all. Likewise in life, even the minutest of advantages counts. There will always be those who have a head start. It is only by what margin. Not only will there be those who only need to swim a shorter distance, but some will battle against the currents, while others are propelled by them. Advantages and opportunities are all that ultimately separate the winners from the losers.

Now let us look at the factors behind Phelps's success.

If winners are born, Phelps was certainly born to win. Nature has given him the physique of a swimming champion: tall and lean with his height close to about 1.93 meters (six feet, four inches). Evidently, at the highest level of competitive swimming, height is of the essence. The overwhelming majority of top male swimmers are well over six feet. Australian two-time Olympic gold medalist in the fifteen-hundred-meter freestyle and one of the world's best-ever long-distance swimmers, Kieren Perkins is 1.94 meters (six feet, four inches), similar in height to Phelps. His countryman Grant Hackett, who is famous for winning the men's fifteen-hundred-meter freestyle race at both the 2000 and 2004 Summer Olympics in Sydney and Athens respectively, is 1.98 meters (six feet, six inches). Winner of five Olympic gold medals, the most won by any Australian, and the first person to win six gold medals in one world championship, Ian Thorpe stands at 1.95 meters (six feet, five inches). Three-time Olympic champion and former world-record holder in the hundred-meter butterfly, Ian Crocker is 1.96 meters (six feet, five inches). Matt Biondi, the three-time US Olympic swimmer who equaled Mark Spitz as the second swimmer to win seven medals in one Olympic Games and a member of the United States Olympic Hall of Fame and International Swimming Hall of Fame, stands at a remarkable two meters (six feet, seven inches) tall. So does Russian Olympic gold medalist Alexander Popov, regarded as one of the greatest sprint freestyle swimmers of all time. Since height and physique are inherited characteristics, your genes pretty much influence your chances of winning a swimming competition. The average height of a male in the United States is 1.78 meters (five feet, ten inches). In comparison, the average height of a male in Vietnam, a country that, to this date, has not produced any world-class swimmers, is only 1.62 meters (five feet, four inches).

In addition to his height, Phelps has exceptionally long arms spanning six feet, seven inches (2.01 meters). They are nearly eighty inches (about three to four inches) longer than his height and are extremely effective as far-reaching propulsive paddles. He has a slim torso and legs, which are relatively short for his body. These physical traits provide him with the advantage of encountering low drag in the water. Drag, which is friction created when a body moves through the water, slows down a swimmer. The drag experienced by each swimmer is different because of their unique body shapes. By experiencing less resistance in the water, a swimmer such as Phelps can go faster and yet uses less energy.

Since 2003, researchers at The George Washington University have studied the mechanics of the kick in aquatic creatures such as dolphins and applied this knowledge to the science of swimming. Dr. Rajat Mittal, a professor at the university whose specialty is in fluid mechanics, and his graduate students have, in collaboration with USA Swimming, created simulations of elite swimmers. Their objective is to discover how and why their kick works so effectively. Mittal has studied the underwater video of Phelps. With a US shoe size of fourteen, Phelps is famous for his big feet, which have the same effect of someone swimming with a pair of flippers. Obviously, the use of flippers is prohibited in any competition, unless the flippers and your feet are one and the same. Another unusual trait is his ankles. His hyper-mobile ankles allow him to extend them beyond the point of a ballet dancer. Phelps's use of the dolphin kick, the undulating, wavelike motion he makes underwater, is said to be one of the many contributing factors to his success. A bigger foot provides more thrust, and Phelps's enormous feet certainly help. Mittal has observed that these attributes allow Phelps to whip his feet for maximum thrust through the water and concluded that this flexibility provides Phelps with a tremendous advantage.

In a nutshell, Phelps's unique physical attributes make him the perfect swimming machine. With sufficient training and the right techniques, it was only a question of winning at which level and what was the color of the medal.

But is it true that whether your family is rich or poor is ultimately immaterial? The pool itself is obviously not capable of bias. However, which country you come from and what social class you belong to matters. Look at the list of swimming champions, and you will find them hailing mostly from countries such as the United States, Australia, Great Britain, Germany, South Africa, Japan, and China. Still others come from France, Italy, Russia, Hungary, Spain, and New Zealand. It is obvious that these are affluent nations where swimming is a well-developed sport with adequate training facilities and world-class coaches.

How many swimming champions are from developing countries? In the Delhi 2010 Commonwealth Games, a twenty-three-year-old Kenyan made history when he won the men's fifty-meter butterfly event at the SPM Swimming Complex. The Nairobi-born six-footer who specializes in butterfly and freestyle sprints had previously won in Universiade, All-Africa Games, and African Championships, and reached the final at the Olympics, World Championships, and Short Course World Championships. As a holder of African, Universiade, and Olympic records, he has made many achievements that are unprecedented in the history of Kenyan swimming. Winning the first-ever Commonwealth Games swimming medal for his country was a remarkable feat because he went head to head against swimming giants Australian Geoffrey Huegill and South African Roland Schoeman and prevailed. Huegill, a previous record holder in the event, is a multiple Olympic, World, and Commonwealth medalist. Schoeman was, at the time of the event, the world record holder in the short-course fifty-meter freestyle and had an illustrious career winning many gold, silver, and bronze medals in the Commonwealth, Olympics, and FINA World Aquatics Championships for freestyle and butterfly events. Compared to Australia and South Africa, which are superpowers in competitive swimming, Kenya was merely a minnow.

In another part of the same continent, thousands of miles south of the arid grasslands and touristy game reserves of Kenya, another African, this time a woman, became a world swimming sensation when she won three medals, including a gold, at the 2004 Athens Olympics. She is arguably the most successful Olympic participant ever from the former British crown colony named after the mysterious stone ruins of a twelfth-century kingdom. In the 2008 Beijing Olympics, she surpassed her previous medal tally by winning one gold and three silver. Paul Chingoka, head of her country's Olympic Committee, called her "our national treasure." Born in the capital city of Harare, she was honored by her country's infamous head of state, President Robert Mugabe, who described her as "a golden girl" and awarded her US$100,000 for her achievement in the 2008 Olympics. The Kenyan is Jason Edward Dunford, and the Zimbabwean is Kirsty Leigh Coventry. Both belong to their countries' tiny minority. Is this merely a coincidence?

Like many sub-Saharan African countries, Kenya and Zimbabwe have an overwhelmingly indigenous black African population. Whites, mostly descendants of British settlers who arrived there when they were still colonies of an empire governed from London, comprise merely a small fraction of 1 percent. Colloquially known as mzungu in Swahili, whites number only thirty thousand out of Kenya's approximately forty million people. Zimbabwe had one of the largest white populations in southern Africa, with a peak of 296,000 in 1975. Back then it was still known as Rhodesia, named after Cecil Rhodes, the founder of the diamond company De Beers. His legacy is still remembered today by South Africa's Rhodes University and the prestigious Rhodes Scholarships, a postgraduate award to study at the University of Oxford. After Ian Smith's white minority government succumbed to international pressure and relinquished control to black majority rule in 1980, its white population dwindled. The current estimated population of less than thirty thousand continues to shrink, exacerbated by the threats of violence that often came hand in hand with the forced acquisitions of white-owned farms by the Mugabe government for redistribution since 2000.

People of European descent are merely a speck of Africa's one billion people. So why are the world-class swimmers from this continent predominantly white? This phenomenon is not unique to Africa. One of the finalists at the 2010 Commonwealth Games men's fifty-meter butterfly, where Dunford emerged as winner, was Papua New Guinea's Ryan Pini. Born in 1981 in Port Moresby, Ryan John Pini is a two-time Olympic swimmer who served as his country's flag-bearer at the 2008 Olympics. Pini, the first swimmer ever from Papua New Guinea to reach an Olympic final, has also previously made world headlines in his own right. His greatest achievement was at the 2006 Commonwealth Games, when he edged out favorite Michael Klim of Australia and Moss Burmester of New Zealand to win the men's hundred-meter butterfly. The 1.93-meter (six-foot, four-inch) swimmer became the second individual from Papua New Guinea to win an individual gold medal and the first-ever swimming medal at any Olympic or Commonwealth Games.

Like Kenya and Zimbabwe, Papua New Guinea is a Commonwealth country with English as an official language. Located in the southwestern corner of the Pacific Ocean, it is one of the least explored countries in the world. Its population of seven million consists overwhelmingly of indigenous Papuans, who speak 820 languages and survive on primitive subsistence-based agriculture as their ancestors have done for thousands of years. Until the twentieth century, some of the tribes living in the interior still had little contact with the civilized world and have the fearsome reputation as cannibals.

Do whites have a genetic predisposition to excel as swimmers? Undoubtedly competitive swimming at the international level has always been a white-dominated sport with a few people of other races making headlines from time to time. However, although few in number, there are black gold medalists in swimming. But why are they not from Africa?

Born on the Caribbean island of Curaçao, then part of the Netherland Antilles, Enith Brigitha learned to swim in the sea. She had the good fortune to emigrate to the Netherlands with her mother. Becoming the top Dutch swimmer of her time, Brigitha won twenty-one national titles in various events between 1973 and 1979, including the Dutch hundred-meter freestyle title seven times consecutively. Representing Netherlands in international meets, she won seven medals in European Championships, four in World Championships, and two in the 1976 Olympics. Also hailing from a former Dutch colony, Anthony Nesty became the second black athlete after Brigitha to win an Olympic medal in swimming. In 1988, Nesty made the smallest sovereign nation in South America proud when he beat favorite Matt Biondi for the gold medal in the hundred-meter butterfly event at the Seoul Olympics. Becoming the only Olympic winner from Suriname, Nesty out-touched Biondi by a slim, razor-thin 0.01 second. There appears to be no shortage of dramatic finishes at the pool. Edging out your closest competitor by a fraction of a second seems to be a staple feature of swimming competitions. To commemorate his historic performance, the government of this ethnically diverse nation issued stamps and coins in his honor. It is not always that a relatively obscure country with less than half a million people can beat the world's most powerful nation with a population of more than 200 million. Barely a decade ago, Suriname was a Dutch colony with an uncertain future. In the years preceding its independence in 1975, nearly one third of its population emigrated because they had lacked confidence that Suriname would be viable as an independent country. With Suriname's population consisting mainly of descendants of African slaves or Asian indentured workers, Nesty's achievements became a source of pride that united his countrymen.

While Suriname itself has not produced many famous sports people, emigrants of Surinamese origin and their descendants, who number more than a quarter of a million in the Netherlands, are well represented in the sporting life of this affluent Western European nation. Several prominent members of the Dutch national football team are of Surinamese origin. They include Ruud Gullit, Frank Rijkaard, Patrick Kluivert, and Edgar Davids, who are named in the FIFA 100, the list of the "greatest living footballers" selected by Brazilian football legend Pele.

Another black Olympic swimmer is Cullen Jones. Team USA had to win the four hundred-meter freestyle men's relays in order for Phelps to achieve the unprecedented eight gold medal tally in the Beijing Olympics. In one of the most exciting relays ever, the team completed in a world-record time of three minutes, 8.24 seconds. Born in the Bronx, Jones became the second African-American to win an Olympic swimming gold medal and an inspiration to black youth across the country to take up that sport. In the 2009 US National Championships in Indianapolis, he set the American record in the fifty-meter freestyle.

So let us come back to our earlier question. Why are there hardly any black swimming champions from Africa? Simple. Any competitive swimmer with a serious chance of winning requires hours of rigorous training in the water on an almost daily basis. They would need access to a suitable body of water to train in. It should be a safe environment with similar conditions and dimensions as the pools they would be competing in. A river, pond, lake, dam, or disused mining pool is far from ideal. In affluent and developed countries such as the United States, Australia, Great Britain, and Germany, pools are located throughout the country and are easily accessible and affordable to the public. Coaching is available for children in most public pools, allowing many to learn swimming at a young age. The affordability and accessibility to swimming pools, together with the availability of coaching programs, mean that one does not have to be fairly wealthy to take up swimming. Consequently, thousands of children from all social backgrounds swim competitively, and the national teams of these countries have a much larger pool of talent to select from. In countries such as Kenya, Zimbabwe, and Papua New Guinea, on the other hand, the average person has issues to contend with that are far more important than access to swimming facilities. According to CIA's *The World Fact Book 2010*, the population living below the national poverty line for Kenya is 50 percent, Papua New Guinea 37 percent, and Zimbabwe 58 percent. All three countries are also rife with violent crime, usually a direct correlation with poverty. Kenya and Zimbabwe both have problems with high rates of unemployment, large numbers of HIV cases, and poor hygiene, as well as limited access to healthcare, clean water, and affordable education. A significant percentage of the residents of Nairobi, Jason Dunford's hometown, live in slums. Nairobi's Kibera is said to be the second largest slum in Africa. With a reputation of being a dangerous city, the capital of Kenya has the nickname "Nairobbery." Zimbabwe's crime rate has skyrocketed with the economic and food crises sparked by the land confiscations that begun in 2000. The hyperinflation and mass unemployment have culminated in a humanitarian crisis. How can the construction of sports facilities be a priority when your country has many more pressing needs?

In the poorer countries, it is the more affluent segment of the population that can afford to pursue sports, especially those requiring facilities such as a swimming pool. Whites happen to be well represented among the affluent in Kenya, Zimbabwe, and Papua New Guinea. When independence was achieved by many African nations in the 1960s and 1970s, many settlers of European descent departed, but others remained to form a small but influential minority. In Kenya, the prominent Cholmondeley family of English aristocratic origin, for example, still possesses over 100,000 acres of land in the Rift Valley. Virtually all white Kenyans economically belong to the middle and upper classes with high-income occupations such as game ranchers, tour operators, professionals, and entrepreneurs. One such person is Jason Dunford's father, who is the chairman of the Tamarind Group, which owns the world-famous Carnivore Restaurant. Dunford's mother comes from the family who founded the Block Hotels. Like in Kenya, most whites in Zimbabwe are well-to-do people. This at least was the case until Robert Mugabe's regime began the seizure of white-owned farms under his land reform program. In the 1970s, a few thousand white commercial farmers owned and cultivated tobacco, cotton, and maize on more than 70 percent of Zimbabwe's arable land.

This observation is not exclusive to swimming but appears to hold true for other sports. Let's look at golf and tennis as examples. Both sports have for a long time been perceived as white-dominated sports until the emergence of Arthur Ashe in the 1980s and Tiger Woods and Serena and Venus Williams in the 1990s. Golf and tennis are historically associated with the more affluent segment of society, and members of the working class found it expensive to have access to golf courses and tennis courts. In many poorer nations, this remains the case. Who are the golfers and tennis stars from Africa?

Zimbabwe's tiny white population has produced more than its fair share of world-renowned sportspeople. In tennis, there are the siblings Byron, Cara and Wayne Black, and Andrew Pattison. Golf enthusiasts would be familiar with the names of Mark McNulty, Nick Price, and Brendon de Jonge. Zimbabwe also had a mostly white world-class cricket team in the 1980s, which included stars such as Andy Flower, Grant Flower, Alistair Campbell, John Bredenkamp, and Heath Streak. The correlation between affluence and participation in certain sports is apparent. For example, when golf and tennis were a sport for the middle and upper classes, the top competitors were not only whites. They were mostly affluent whites. Tiger Woods was born in the suburban city of Cypress, California, and began learning golf in affluent Orange County. It is no surprise that prominent black tennis players, too, hail from affluent countries. France has Yannick Noah, Gianni Mina, Gael Monfils, and Jo-Wilfried Tsonga, while the United States has Donald Young, Chanda Rubin, Zina Garrison, Lori McNeil, and the siblings MaliVai and Mashona Washington, to name but a few other than Ashe and the Williams sisters.

There is no question that champions start early and are introduced to their sport at an incredibly young age. Tiger Woods started golf at the tender age of two. Even before the age of three, Woods took part in the under-age-ten category of a golf competition in Cypress, California. At age five, he was featured in *Golf Digest* and on ABC's *That's Incredible*. By the time he was eight, he won the nine-to-ten boys' event at the Junior World Golf Championships. Woods was the winner of the Junior World Golf Championships six times. The 2010 documentary *Tiger Woods: Rise and Fall* provides interesting insights into Woods's secret to greatness. Much of his success was attributed to his father, a golf enthusiast, who was determined that his offspring would be a golf champion even before he was born. Serena Williams started playing tennis at only age five. This was late in comparison to the head start tennis superstar Steffi Graf got. Her father, a tennis enthusiast, introduced her to the sport at the age of three by teaching her how to swing a wooden racket. At age four, Graf was playing on a tennis court. A year later, she played her first tournament. Her father controlled her schedule during her childhood and teenage years. Steffi

Graf went on to win twenty-two Grand Slam singles titles in her remarkable career. Jason Dunford started swimming at the age five and was soon competing. At age thirteen, Dunford was sent to the United Kingdom, where he trained under coach Peter O'Sullivan, a former British swimmer. By 2004, Dunford was competing at various World Championship events.

By contrast, Phelps only began swimming at the age of seven. However, at age eleven, he trained under Bowman, a tough coach, who pushed Phelps to swim at least fifty miles a week. Bowman has commented that children who begin training at that age are able to increase the size of their hearts and lungs in a manner not possible for those who begin training at a later age. A larger heart and lungs gives them the advantage of having a bigger aerobic engine. Phelps's grueling training meant that he was in the pool five hours a day every day of the week, leaving him little time to do anything else. With few exceptions, Phelps swam every day, including on his birthdays and Christmas. Like with Tiger Woods, his intensive schedule meant that he had to forego many of the experiences he should have enjoyed during his childhood and teenage years. At age ten, Phelps became the national record holder for his age group. At age fifteen, he became the youngest male to qualify for the United States Olympics swim team in sixty-eight years. Before his sixteenth birthday, Phelps broke the world record in the two-hundred-meter butterfly event at the trials for the 2001 World Aquatics Championships. By starting early, champions like Phelps accumulate valuable experience by participating in many international competitions years before they make front-page news with their gold medals.

World champions have a head start because they were introduced to the sports at such an early age that it would have been impossible for them as youngsters to make such decisions themselves. Some were just toddlers. By the time they were older, they just carried on doing what they were good at. People enjoy doing what they excel in and that which gives them the most significance. Michael Phelps is so at home in the water and loves to swim that he told an interviewer, "My job is to be in the water and swim." It was his older sisters, Whitney and Hilary, both competitive swimmers, who introduced him to swimming. Whitney was a member of the 1995 World Championship swim team. In the case of Jason Dunford, his father was the vice chairman of the Kenya Swimming Federation and the patron of the Nairobi Amateur Swimming Association. David, his younger brother, also swims for Kenya. For the vast majority of sports champions, their families were a major factor in their success. It is no wonder that sportspeople have siblings who also excel in the same sport.

All great swimmers have had great coaches at some point of their careers. Raw talent only takes you so far. Many foreign swimmers were trained in the United States, including Kirsty Coventry, Jason Dunford, and Cavic, the Serbian swimmer who almost sunk Phelps's hopes of making history. Anthony Nesty trained in Bolles School, the renowned center in Jacksonville, Florida, which has produced so many elite world-class swimmers, including the hundred-meter backstroke Olympic gold medalist Martin Lopez-Zubero Purcell and his brother David, an Olympic bronze medalist in the hundred-meter butterfly. Although Ryan Pini swims for Papua New Guinea, he trains primarily in Brisbane, Australia, and competes for the Yeronga Park Swim Club.

Last but not least, the country you represent makes a difference especially in team events. Of the eight gold medals Phelps won in Beijing, three were in relays:

August 11, 2008 - 4x100-meter freestyle relay with Garrett Weber-Gale, Cullen Jones, and Jason Lezak

August 13, 2008 - 4×200-meter freestyle relay with Ryan Lochte, Ricky Berens, and Peter Vanderkaay

August 17, 2008 - 4×100-meter medley relay with Aaron Peirsol, Brendan Hansen, and Jason Lezak

If Phelps had swum for Zimbabwe, Kenya, or Papua New Guinea, winning a gold medal in a relay event would have certainly been impossible. Only countries such as France, Australia, Italy, Sweden, Canada, South Africa, Great Britain, Germany, Japan, Russia, Hungary, and New Zealand had strong men's swimming teams that could challenge the United States in one or more of the relay events.

"You can't put a limit on anything. The more you dream, the further you get," Michael Phelps famously said. Phelps's incredible mental strength has been credited as one of the key elements to his success. But it takes much more than just determination, hard work, and positive thinking. Even winners need help.

CHAPTER 2:
PERFECT TIMING

Arguably the most renowned Frenchman, Napoleon is regarded as one of the greatest military geniuses of all time. His strategies are studied in military academies across the world. His victories are featured in books and documentaries on historical battles. Yet one of his greatest legacies is the creation of the Napoleonic Code, which forms the basis of the legal systems in many countries occupied by the French during the Napoleonic Wars. Long after his defeat, countries such as Italy, the Netherlands, Belgium, Spain, and Portugal have adopted his code and kept it to this day and even passed it on to their former colonies in Africa and the Americas. A man ahead of his times, he emancipated Jews in areas under his control in an era when anti-Semitism was prevalent. Napoleon was a Corsican. His homeland was an island west of Italy and south of France, where the inhabitants, known for their vendettas, speak a Romance language related to Italian. Christened as Napoleone di Buonaparte, he changed his name in his twenties to a more French-sounding one, perhaps thinking it would serve him better.

The future emperor of the French was born the second of eight children on August 15, 1769, in his ancestral home, Casa Buonaparte. The modest four-story mansion is still preserved in Ajaccio, Corsica's capital and largest city, where his memory is visible everywhere in statues and street names. Since 1347, the Most Serene Republic of Genoa, one of the many states that would later form modern Italy, has governed Corsica. But in 1729, a strong independence movement began to take shape and gained momentum in the following decades.

In November 1755, Corsican freedom fighters under Pasquale Paoli were strong enough to proclaim the Corsican Republic as a sovereign nation. By the 1760s, after years of conflict, the rebels were so successful that the Genoese had lost control of most of the Mediterranean island. Unable to extend their control beyond the coastal towns and citadels, the Genoese cleverly sold Corsica to the Kingdom of France under the Treaty of Versailles concluded on May 15, 1768. Napoleon was born just one year after the acquisition.

On May 8 and 9, 1769, French forces under Comte de Vaux, a seasoned military commander, crushed the Corsicans under Carlo Salicetti, Paoli's second in command, in the Battle of Ponte Novu. The battle, which was just months before Napoleon's birth, effectively put an end to the self-proclaimed Corsican Republic and paved the way to France's total subjugation of the island. Corsica became part of France. Instead of being a citizen of the small and obscure Genoese Republic, Napoleon grew up having as much right to call himself a Frenchman as a Breton from the rainy northwest Celtic fringe or an Occitan-speaker from Provence. Today, although the island with a population of 300,000 is administered in the same manner as any other region of France, there are still nationalistic groups among the Corsicans calling for autonomy or even full independence. It is Corsica's greatest son that has cemented its link with France.

Although not immensely wealthy, the Bonapartes were affluent. The family was descended from minor Italian nobility who arrived in Corsica in the sixteenth century. They had originated from Liguria, the same region of Italy where the maritime republic of Genoa is situated. His father, Carlo Buonaparte, was Corsica's representative to the court of King Louis XVI. Napoleon's upper-middle-class background gave him many opportunities that were not afforded to the common people of Europe who lived in that era. This was significant because it allowed Napoleon to enroll in a school in Autun, France, to study French and subsequently gain acceptance into the military academy at Brienne-le-Chateau. Thereafter, he was admitted to the elite Ecole Militaire, where he trained to become an artillery officer. Completing a two-year course within the span of a year, he became the first Corsican to graduate from the prestigious military school.

In 1789, there began a decade of social and political upheaval unprecedented in European history. A violent and turbulent chain of events would abolish the monarchy as well as aristocratic privileges. French society went through a radical and traumatic transformation. The ancien regime that ruled France for many centuries collapsed. It was previously unimaginable. The French kings were among the most powerful, magnificent, and wealthiest in Europe.

A number of factors came together to bring about the outbreak of the French Revolution. In 1783, Lakagigar, a volcano situated near the Eldgja canyon in southeastern Iceland, erupted. Lasting over a period of eight months, it was one of the deadliest volcanic eruptions in history, spewing clouds of poisonous hydrofluoric acid and sulfur dioxide compounds. Historians believe that it could have been responsible for the death of six million people. It was estimated that 120 million tons of sulfur dioxide were emitted. Thick haze covered parts of the earth from the sun's rays, resulting in unusual weather conditions and a drop in temperatures in the northern hemisphere. Particularly harsh winters were the result. Crop failures occurred on a

E Ong

massive scale. This in turn caused widespread famine. The shortage of grain caused the price of bread to skyrocket. This led to starvation as bread formed one of the main diet of the peasants. The cities were overcrowded with destitute peasants. A hungry man is an angry man. In the two years preceding the French Revolution, starvation was particularly severe, sparking the unrest known as the "bread riots."

Another event that became a major contributing factor occurred across the Atlantic. The American Revolutionary War, which began in 1775, is perhaps better known as the American War of Independence. Britain's thirteen North American colonies united and fought for their independence from the British Empire. Unlike the wars of liberation waged by the indigenous peoples of Africa and Asia against their European colonial masters in the twentieth century, it was not a war between nationalities. A large number of American colonists were of British heritage and considered themselves subjects of the British Crown. Many prominent colonials, including George Washington, had served in the British military campaigns against the empire's enemies. It was a series of unpopular legislation passed by Britain that culminated in the declaration of independence.

Influenced by ideas of the Enlightenment, the colonials objected to the authority of the Parliament in London to enact and impose laws on them on the basis that none of the thirteen colonies were represented in the British legislature. On September 5, 1774, representatives of the self-governing colonies met at the First Continental Congress in Philadelphia to jointly petition King George III to intervene with Parliament on their behalf. At this stage, the colonies continued to affirm their loyalty to the British monarch. Britain responded by dispatching troops to establish greater control. On May 10, 1775, the Second Continental Congress was held in Philadelphia to discuss the formation of a united front to defend themselves against the British military forces if the need arose. Additional petitions to George III to intervene with Parliament resulted in Congress being declared as traitors and the colonies to be in a state of rebellion. The thirteen colonies responded by renouncing their allegiance to the British monarch and formally declaring their independence as the United States of America on July 4, 1776.

The political basis of the American Revolution was that the legitimacy of the British Parliament to govern them without representation ought to be rejected as this violated the "Rights of Englishmen." Ultimately, the hostile stance taken by Britain resulted in the colonialists repudiating their loyalty altogether. The seventeenth century had been the Age of Reason or Age of Rationality. More philosophies and ideas subsequently developed, and the eighteenth century became known as the Age of Enlightenment. It was an era of great significance in the cultural, intellectual, and scientific realms of the Western world. A host of philosophers, thinkers, scientists, economists, and political leaders developed ideas that at times were divergent and conflicting. It was the Enlightenment that became the ideological movement behind the American Revolution with the concepts of liberalism, democracy, and republicanism. The English philosopher John Locke's ideas on liberty was a major influence behind the revolution. So was the French philosopher Jean-Jacques Rousseau's theory of social contract. And it was Rousseau's philosophy that influenced the founding fathers to believe that the "natural rights"

E Ong

of man included the right of the people to overthrow their leaders should they betray the historic "Rights of Englishmen."

The American Revolutionary War was an ideological war. It was fought between those adhering to the ideas of the Enlightenment and those who still believed in the right of the king to exercise his unfettered powers. The belligerents were republicans on one side and royalists on the other. The American Revolutionary War was as divisive as the American Civil War fought almost a century later. Families were divided. Although Benjamin Franklin became a founding father of the United States, his son, William, the last Loyalist governor of New Jersey, took up arms against his countrymen fighting for the revolutionary cause. Remaining loyal to the crown after the war, William resettled in England and never spoke to his father again. Historians believe that perhaps as high as 20 percent of the population of the American colonies remained loyal to the British monarch and were known as "Loyalists," "Tories," or simply the "King's men." On the side of the American Revolutionaries, quite a fair few were British or at least British-born, including the naval hero John Paul Jones and Major General Horatio Gates, the victor of the Battle of Saratoga. After the war, tens of thousands of Loyalists left for Britain or relocated to the British colonies in the West Indies and Canada.

Between 1756 and 1763, France and Britain fought the Seven Years' War. The outcome was the loss of Quebec and other French colonies in the Caribbean, Africa, and India. Humiliated and deeply resentful about its defeat by the British, France saw the opportunity for revenge with the advent of the American Revolution. Beginning with providing supplies and weapons to the thirteen colonies, it subsequently participated as a combatant by sending thousands of troops to fight in North America. Thanks to the help from the French and Spanish, the American revolutionaries emerged victorious in 1781. The high cost of its participation in the war, however, added to France's enormous financial debt.

The trouble with ideas is that they are contagious and are capable of causing a government's downfall. Like viruses, ideas are transmitted from person to person, simply by being exposed to it. An individual who contracts it himself becomes a carrier. This is shown in other historic events. Jose Rizal, Philippines's national hero who called for reforms in the Spanish colony, was exposed to the philosophies of European thinkers while he studied in Madrid, Paris, and Heidelberg. Mohandas Karamchand Gandhi studied law at University College London and was exposed to the radical ideas of Jeremy Bentham. Gandhi would return to India to become the driving force of an independence movement. His experience in London and South Africa, where he worked briefly as a lawyer, had a profound impact on his political activism. Sun Yat-Sen, the founding father of Republican China, spent many years of his life abroad, including in Hong Kong, Hawaii, the United States, Canada, and Japan. During this time, he became deeply influenced by Western thought and in particular the ideas of Alexander Hamilton and Abraham Lincoln. It was the democratic and republican principles, especially those of the United States, that he was exposed to that shaped him as a revolutionary. Sun's cause was supported and funded by thousands of like-minded Chinese living in the diaspora and exposed to the same ideas. For many periods in China, the emperors had forbidden their subjects to have any interaction with foreigners. They were right.

E Ong

In the same year that Sun's Chinese Revolution took place, Nguyen Sinh Cung, the son of a Vietnamese Confucian scholar, traveled to the United States, where he lived for a while in New York and Boston. It was there that he was influenced by Marcus Garvey, the black nationalist who would one day be the national hero of Jamaica. Nguyen then stayed for a number of years in Britain and France. In Paris he met the French politician Marcel Cachin, who introduced him to communism. When the French Communist Party was formed in 1921, Nguyen became one of its founding members. It is said that he petitioned Woodrow Wilson to provide assistance for the removal of the French from Vietnam and replace it with a nationalist government. Nguyen cited the language and the spirit of the American Declaration of Independence. Unsurprisingly, the petition from this virtually unknown person was ignored. Wilson would not be the last American president who would hear of Nguyen.

In 1923, Nguyen left for Moscow to see for himself the newly established socialist republic in Russia. Finally returning to Vietnam in 1941, he became the leader of the Vietnamese nationalist forces that saw the defeat of the French colonial forces. Soon after, the United States became involved in the Vietnam War, committing more than half a million troops to the conflict by 1969. President Richard Nixon famously said, "North Vietnam cannot defeat the United States." Nevertheless, the United States-backed government of South Vietnam fell in April 1975, and on May 1, its capital, Saigon, was renamed after Nguyen. The formidable Vietnamese Marxist revolutionary leader Nguyen Sinh Cung is better known by his nom de guerre, Ho Chi Minh. Across the border in Cambodia, a young man had obtained a scholarship to study in Paris in 1949. Like with Ho Chi Minh, it was in France that he embraced communism. Together with a number of Cambodian communists educated in France, he led the Khmer Rouge to power in 1975. Known by his pseudonym Pol Pot, he is remembered for the Cambodian genocide.

Many thousands of French troops were sent to fight alongside the American revolutionaries. It is not difficult to imagine that in the course of bleeding and dying for the Americans they would have been exposed to their republican ideas of "equality" and "freedom of the individual" by the revolutionaries whose cause they upheld. They would perhaps also be introduced to the ideas of many philosophers of the Enlightenment who were their countrymen. Among them were Voltaire, Diderot, and Turgot. The success of the American Revolution culminated in the creation of a republic with a representative government responsible to the will of the people. The constitution of the new nation, which was influenced by the thoughts of the famous French political thinker Montesquieu, demonstrated that it was possible for a state to apply the ideas of the Enlightenment. The French war veterans sailed home only to encounter the autocratic nature of their own government. Infected with the revolutionary ideals, the returnees soon began to help spread them among the common people.

Let us now return to France on the eve of the revolution. Louis XVI ascended the throne of France on May 10, 1774. He was barely twenty. The problem was that his predecessor, who was known for his debauchery, had spent extravagantly on Versailles, adding to the heavy expenditures spent on the Seven Years' War. The ill-advised fiscal policies of Louis XV had weakened the treasury and failed to overcome the country's escalating financial problems. France's expenditures continued to surpass its revenues. Thus, Louis XVI not only inherited the crown but a chronic budget deficit. Unfortunately, it was now up to him to pick up the tab. Instead, the debt continued to increase, and there was a failure to curb the downward spiral. In the years preceding the revolution, France was not just facing a major fiscal crisis but was effectively bankrupt. King Louis XVI took the immensely unpopular and unwise step of imposing high taxes on the common people while granting tax exemption to the nobility. In a country already suffering from crop failures and famine, it ultimately became the straw that broke the camel's back.

To find a solution to the country's serious financial problems, a meeting of the Estates-General was summoned and commenced on May 5, 1789. This was a general assembly attended by members of the three estates of the realm, namely the nobility, the clergy, and the common people. The Estates-General had been largely ceremonial, and its last meeting was held more than a century and a half before in 1614. After several weeks of sitting in May and June 1789, the three Estates came to an impasse, as there was bitter disagreement over their respective powers. At its core was the issue of voting. The Third Estate, which in theory represented the common people, had twice the number of delegates as each of the other Estates. However, when the meeting convened, it was announced that each Estate had only one vote. This would mean that despite their superior numbers, the Third Estate could always be outvoted by the other two. Considering this to be undemocratic, the representatives of the Third Estate left and boycotted the meeting. Convening a separate meeting, this National Assembly declared themselves as an assembly of the people. Jacques

Necker, the finance minister, persuaded Louis XVI to attempt to reconcile the squabbling Estates. However, Louis XVI ultimately went along with the advice of the courtiers of his privy council. The Salle des Etats, the hall where the National Assembly met, was closed. Members of the National Assembly responded by meeting on a nearby tennis court. It was here that they made the famous Tennis Court Oath to not separate until France acquired a constitution.

A series of events began to cause tensions to rapidly escalate. On June 11, 1789, Necker, a sympathizer of the Third Estate, was dismissed by Louis XVI on the urging of his enemies, the Comte d'Artois, and other conservative nobles in the king's inner circle. The news of the sacking of the immensely popular Necker resulted in the people of Paris assuming that it was merely a beginning of an action by the monarch against the Assembly. The capital of France was in chaos as riots took place throughout the city. On July 14, with the support of armed French soldiers who shared the revolutionary fervor, a mob attacked the Bastille. The fortress, a symbol of power of the French monarch, fell after several hours of fighting, and Governor Marquis Bernad de Launay was decapitated. His head was fixed on a pike and carried in the streets by the victorious mob. Although the citizens of Paris prepared themselves for an attack, the king, shocked by the violence, backed down. The last thing France needed in such tumultuous times was a weak and indecisive king. And that was exactly what Louis XVI was. At that juncture, he had at his disposal considerable numbers of foreign mercenaries. Many of the troops concentrated in Paris and Versailles were Germans and Swiss, who had little sympathy for the cause compared to ordinary French soldiers. On July 12, when Parisians clashed with the Royal-Allemende, a Calvary regiment consisting of German mercenaries, the troops were ordered to withdraw to avoid a bloodbath.

On October 5, seven thousand women, many of whom worked in the markets of Paris, made the epic march to Versailles to demand a solution to bread shortages. The mob stormed the palace, and the terrified king, who had refused to flee despite his queen's persuasion, became virtually a prisoner of his people. The monarch and his family relocated to Paris the following day, escorted by the mob, which triumphantly carried the severed heads of his guards on pikes. It was too late. In September 1792, France was declared a republic. The following year, King Louis XVI was beheaded.

In April 1793, the government of the new French republic created a board ironically named the Committee of Public Safety. This powerful committee came to be dominated by the eloquent lawyer Maximillien Robespierre. Robespierre became one of the most famous and dominant figures of the French Revolution. His popularity and appeal were derived from his extraordinary oratory skills. His speeches were capable of changing the views of his audience. He was called "The Incorruptible" by his supporters and a blood-thirsty dictator by his opponents. At the trial of Louis XVI in December 1792, Robespierre was one of the chief advocates of the king's execution, arguing that he posed a threat to the republic. After the king lost his head, Robespierre and members of his Jacobin political faction began to move against their rivals within the revolutionary movement. From June 1793 to July 1794, there began one of the most violent periods in French history, which saw the executions of the "enemies of the revolution." It was known as the Reign of Terror, and Robespierre became the driving force behind it, constantly preaching a message that the revolution was under relentless threat from traitors and saboteurs from all quarters, including from within. In June 1793, the members of the powerful Girondist political faction, including their leader, Jacques Pierre Brissot, were purged and sent to the guillotine. Robespierre's uncompromising views resulted in the execution of many of the revolution's staunchest and most influential figures. Another political faction would face the blade. In March 1794, Jacques Hébert and nineteen of his followers were guillotined. This was soon followed by the execution of Georges Danton, Camille Desmoulins, and their allies on April 5. A fellow Jacobin, Danton had also been a member of the Committee of Public Safety and a close colleague of Robespierre.

On July 26, Robespierre made a speech in the National Convention, where he accused some of the members present of plotting against the revolution. While announcing that he had the list of conspirators, he refused to provide them when requested. This proved to be a fatal mistake. Fearing that any of them might be next, the convention promptly ordered the arrest of Robespierre and his staunchest supporters. On July 28, 1794, Robespierre went to the guillotine with his followers. Historians believe that as many as forty thousand people lost their lives in the Reign of Terror before its progenitor, Robespierre, was finally decapitated, lying face up.

The royal institution of France had been destroyed by the revolution. The monarchy and the powerful French aristocracy, which held so many influential positions, had been swept away. Perceived as opponents of the revolution for their loss of privileges, some nobles were executed. Among them was Louis Phillipe II, Duke of Orleans, who met his fate at the "National Razor," as the guillotine was called, despite having declared himself an ardent supporter of the French Revolution. Many others, including Comte d'Artois, fled for their lives and sought refuge in neighboring countries, where they became known as French émigrés. Now only after a short period, the most prominent leaders of French Revolution were gone, too, thanks to Robespierre. Incidentally, Napoleon was detained for two weeks before being released following the fall of Robespierre for being the latter's ally. And what a friend Robespierre was. Robespierre's actions had created a leadership vacuum. The events had unwittingly set the stage for the charismatic Napoleon to fill that vacuum.

As soon as the French Revolution started in 1791, rulers of European states were concerned with the upheavals caused by the common people rising up against their king. By 1792, the new republic found itself at war with the combined armies of Austria, Prussia, Hesse, and Sardinia. By 1793, revolutionary France was also at war with Spain, Portugal, Britain, and the Dutch Republic. As it was, the French army already had to contend with putting out rebellions by counter-revolutionary forces across the country. Now it also had to scramble to recruit, train, and arm hundreds of thousands of Frenchmen to defend the country's territory from foreign invaders. France desperately needed a savior. It was facing a peril of unparalleled magnitude since the Muslim invasion of 732. Francois de la Rochefoucauld once said, "Nature creates ability. Luck provides it with opportunity." Virtually all the major states of Europe were in a coalition against France. It was this climate that presented the perfect opportunity for Napoleon to showcase his brilliance.

The revolution had done away with foreign mercenaries in the French army. This, of course, had no effect on Napoleon. He was French. Many of the aristocrats who monopolized the top positions in the French army were gone. Napoleon was not a duke, marquis, comte, vicomte, or baron and was not perceived as a threat to the revolution. The commanders of French forces in the preceding years, such as Charles, Duke of Rohan in the Seven Years' War, and Marquis de Lafayette, comte de Rochambeau and comte de Grasse in the American Revolutionary War, held the highest titles of nobility and came from distinguished pedigree. Although the able and experienced Marquis de Lafayette was sympathetic to the revolutionary cause, he was dismissed of his command and declared a traitor by the National Assembly.

In September 1785, Napoleon served as a second lieutenant in an artillery regiment in southern France when the French Revolution broke out. In 1793, with the support of a fellow Corsican, Napoleon was given the command of an artillery detachment at the siege of port of Toulon. The French revolutionary forces were up against the citizens of Toulon, who were in open rebellion against the republic with the support of considerable numbers of British troops who had landed. It was Napoleon's role in the capture of the city that resulted in his being noticed by the leaders of the revolution. Promoted to brigadier-general, Napoleon was only twenty-four. He was subsequently put in charge of France's Army of Italy. This was only the beginning of his rise to prominence. Among his many conquests, one that was noteworthy occurred in 1797, when the forces of the Corsican-born commander occupied the Most Serene Republic of Genoa and got rid of the elites who governed the state throughout its history. In one of the many strange twists of history, Genoa was annexed to Napoleon's France in 1805.

Napoleon's campaigns ended in spectacular victories, surpassing by far those of previous French commanders. The Italian peninsula, the Low Countries, and most territories west of the Rhine fell to his armies. After the untimely end of Robespierre and the fall of the Jacobins, control of the French state was assumed by the Directory. Consisting of members who were unscrupulous, dissolute, shameless, and weak, the Directory was understandably unpopular with the people. None had the strength of character of the initial leaders of the French Revolution. Finally, in 1799, Napoleon overthrew the Directory and assumed power.

If Napoleon had been born two decades earlier, he might not have been an officer in the French army. Perhaps he might have been no more than a freedom fighter like Paoli, forgotten by all except for a handful of students of eighteenth-century European history. Had he been born a decade later, he would have been too young to have taken advantage of the leadership vacuum or to prove himself as a commander in the French Revolutionary Wars.

There were at least two points in his life when, if Napoleon had chosen a different path, his destiny would have been altered. As a young military officer, Napoleon remained privately a fervent Corsican nationalist. In May 1789, he wrote to the Corsican leader Pasquale Paoli, pledging his support, saying, "...As the nation was perishing I was born. Thirty thousand Frenchmen were vomited on to our shores, drowning the throne of liberty in waves of blood..." Fortunately for Napoleon, the two men eventually fell out. Paoli was so influential in Corsica that the Bonaparte family had to flee to France. The French, however, ultimately defeated the Corsican nationalists, and Paoli lived in exile in England until his death. The other quirky fact of history is that Napoleon at one point considered joining the British navy. This was an era when sailors of various nationalities were welcomed. In the end, he chose instead to become an officer in the French military. Years later, when Napoleon's forces dominated the European continent, the British navy reigned supreme in the seas. The British navy would prove to be a thorn in his side, sinking Napoleon's fleet in his Egyptian Campaign. In 1805, the French suffered a resounding defeat at the hands of the British navy at the Battle of Trafalgar, forcing Napoleon to abandon his plans to launch an invasion of his nemesis, Britain.

The French Revolution was the event where the destinies and fates of Louis XVI and Napoleon intertwined. The former had the misfortune of inheriting a bankrupt nation exacerbated by an extraordinary famine caused by a particularly severe natural disaster. As a king in the Age of Enlightenment, he had to face popular revolutionary ideas not encountered by his predecessors in the aftermath of the American Revolution. This combination of circumstances created the perfect storm. On the other hand, the Bonapartes became French at the right moment. The family's moderate affluence meant that Napoleon would not be branded as an enemy of the revolution, yet it afforded him a solid education that allowed him to become a military officer. The occurrence of the French Revolution was made easier by a weak king, who failed to nip it in the bud by unleashing his foreign mercenaries. With the aristocrats gone from the top officer ranks, opportunities were aplenty for qualified men such as Napoleon to fill such positions. With the many battles as a consequence of the French Revolution, Napoleon could ask for no better opportunities to showcase his military brilliance. After the abolishment of the monarchy, Robespierre eliminated all of the prominent personalities of the French Revolution. On December 2, 1804, Napoleon took the crown in his hands and crowned himself Emperor Napoleon I. It was symbolically apt. There was in fact nobody left who could stop him.

On June 28, 1914, the heir apparent to the throne of the Austro-Hungarian Empire and his wife were assassinated during a visit to Sarajevo. The man who pulled the trigger was only nineteen years old. Too young to receive the death penalty, he was sentenced to twenty years in prison. His deed, however, would have repercussions of an enormous magnitude. Although there were already simmering political tensions between the major European powers, it was this assassination that became the immediate trigger of the First World War.

On July 4, 1918, Mehmed VI Wahid ed-din ascended the throne of the Ottoman Empire. His reign would be a short one. The Ottomans had made the mistake of entering the First World War on the wrong side. During the war, British, Australian, and New Zealander troops had attempted to capture Istanbul. The Gallipoli campaign that took place between 1915 and 1916 was a disaster for the Allies, and it was in this battle that an Ottoman officer by the name of Mustafa made a name for himself. Subsequently taking part in a number of successful offensives against the Russian army, Mustafa's rise in the Turkish military was meteoric. By March 1917, Mustafa was promoted to be the overall commander of the Second Army. With the Russians withdrawing from the war as a result of a revolution at home, Mustafa assumed command of the Seventh Army and fought in Palestine and Syria. Although the troops under Mustafa performed superbly in the military engagements, the First World War ended in defeat for the Central Powers. Anatolia was partitioned and occupied by British, French, Italian, and Greek forces.

In November 1918, Mustafa returned to an Istanbul occupied by foreign troops. This was the first and only time such an event happened since the Turks conquered the city more than 550 years before. When a treaty was signed to partition the Ottoman Empire, Turkish nationalists found in Mustafa Kemal a dynamic leader and rallied behind him. Like Napoleon, Mustafa's capabilities as a superb military commander and charisma as a statesman would be essential ingredients in his assumption of power. From 1921 to 1922, Turkish forces with Mustafa as its commander in chief drove foreign occupiers out of the country, culminating with the recapture of modern-day Izmir from the Greek army on September 9, 1922. Mustafa Kemal's successful military campaigns ensured that Turkey would remain an independent nation, earning the gratitude of his countrymen. Born in Salonika, Greece, to a working class ethnic Albanian father, Mustafa Kemal became known as Ataturk, "father of the Turks." Under his leadership, the country transformed into a modern secular nation through a series of political and economic reforms. The United Nations honored Mustafa by declaring 1981, the centennial of his birth, the Ataturk Year.

As the founder of modern Turkey, Mustafa Kemal left an imprint that is present everywhere in the country. Istanbul's international airport, the country's largest stadium, a dam on the Euphrates River, and a bridge over the Golden Horn are among the many built to commemorate him. His name is not only seen in memorials and street names in almost every city and town in Turkey but also in other countries as diverse as Australia, Netherlands, Dominican Republic, Pakistan, Bangladesh, India, Italy, Israel, and New Zealand. In his homeland, his portrait is in most public buildings and his face on the banknotes.

Opportunities are ever present. They lie in wait for the right moment to present itself to the next Napoleon.

CHAPTER 3:
EVEN GENIUSES NEED A LITTLE HELP

"I have not failed. I've just found ten thousand ways that won't work." These are the powerful words of the man who created the electrical light bulb after countless unsuccessful attempts. One of the most prolific inventors in history, Thomas Edison holds 1,093 patents in the United States alone with many patents in Britain and other European countries. His success has been widely used as one of the classic examples by motivational speakers and writers throughout the globe to inspire their audiences. After all, who would be crazy enough to carry on after the nine thousandth, nine hundredth, and ninety-ninth attempt? The lesson learned from the American inventor is to be relentless in the pursuit of one's goals and never give up. Persevere and have faith in oneself, and success is inevitable. If you are undaunted by your failures, you will prevail in the end. Inspiring stories such as Edison's are very persuasive. While perseverance seems to be the hallmark or conspicuous characteristic of every successful person whose story we have heard, is that all it takes?

In Moscow's Pushkin Museum of Fine Arts is an oil painting called *The Red Vineyard*. After the Russian Revolution, the newly established communist regime had confiscated and nationalized the art collection of a wealthy businessman, and this piece was one of them. It is relatively unknown compared to other works of the artist, such as *Portrait of Dr. Gatchet*, *Portrait of Joseph Roulin*, *Irises*, *A Wheatfield with Cypresses*, and *Vase with Fifteen Sunflowers*. Yet this painting is significant as it was the only known piece sold by the artist during his lifetime. It embodied the artist's dream and ambition to become an accomplished painter someday. Today, it is this same hope that keeps the dreams of thousands of aspiring actors in Hollywood alive while waiting tables and performing various odd jobs in the meantime.

On July 27, 1890, a failed painter shot himself in the chest with a revolver in Auvers-sur-Ouise, France. At thirty-seven, a man his age would have been expected to have firmly established himself in a meaningful profession and be financially self-sustaining. A prolific artist, he had produced more than two thousand works before his suicide. Yet at the time of his death, few knew or appreciated his work. For most of his adulthood, the unemployed Dutchman had suffered from severe depression resulting largely from a series of rejections. By all accounts he was a failure. His stubbornness or perhaps misplaced confidence in his own talent had caused him to squander away the productive years of his life. Consequently, at his deathbed, he had nothing to his name but canvasses of unwanted paintings. He had no family of his own. As a young man, he was madly in love with a widowed relative. When she refused to see him, he held his hand in the flame of a lamp in an act of desperation, pleading, "Let me see her for as long as I can keep my hand in the flame." Despite this incredible gesture, his marriage proposal was flatly rejected because of his inability to financially support himself, let alone a family. He was shunned by his parents, and only his brother was by his side as he gasped his last breath. On July 29, 1890, twenty-nine hours after his self-inflicted injury, a passion that once burned brightly was finally extinguished. Tragically, his supposed last words were, "The sadness will last forever." He persevered until he could persevere no more.

It was not that his works were never displayed in exhibitions. Critics and art dealers in important art shows in Paris and Brussels saw them. Not only did his art receive little positive attention; at times they were even publicly insulted. When his unhappy life, which was filled with anxiety and frequent bouts of mental illness, ended, he was still virtually unknown. His friend's sister, who was known to support struggling and poor artists, bought *The Red Vineyard*, the only painting he ever sold. Vincent van Gogh died a frustrated and bitter man. His legacy, however, is immense.

Hailed as one of the greatest painters ever, van Gogh's influence on twentieth-century art is enormous. While van Gogh died a pauper, his works, together with those of Pablo Picasso, are among the most expensive art to be sold. *The Portrait of Dr. Gatchet, Portrait of Joseph Roulin, Irises, A Wheatfield with Cypresses,* and *Vase with Fifteen Sunflowers* top a very long list of priceless paintings created by the pastor's son from Zundert. In 1990, the *Portrait of Dr. Gachet* was auctioned for $82.5 million.

It takes tremendous courage to persevere. But it takes an equal amount of courage to realize that after so much has been expended, you simply do not have what it takes. Van Gogh's life story beckons us to ask some important questions. How can so many experienced art dealers be so blind? Is it not apparent that these are the works of a genius? When do we stop persevering? When should we finally realize that we will never be the next American Idol or the next Hollywood star? In the case of van Gogh, fortunately, someone had faith in his work and refrained from destroying it.

In 1979, a young man left Taiwan to pursue a degree in the United States. He was following the footsteps of hundreds of thousands from all across the globe to obtain an American education. There was nothing extraordinary about his background. He was born on October 23, 1954, in Chaochou, an agricultural region in the south of the country. His parents were originally from the Chinese mainland. In the immediate aftermath of World War II, the world's most populous country saw a few years of intense warfare between the Soviet-backed communist forces under Mao Zedong and Chiang Kai Shek's Nationalists. When the Nationalists were defeated in 1949, Chiang retreated to Taiwan, relocating his capital from Nanking to Taipei, the island's largest city. There, Chiang's government, which brought with it the country's gold and foreign currency reserves, continued to maintain its claim of sovereignty over the whole of China.

Approximately two million Nationalist army personnel and Kuomintang party members, as well as intellectual and business people, departed the Chinese mainland with Chiang. Among them were the parents of the young man. Their family name was Lee, a surname so common among the Chinese that by the end of the twentieth century it has far surpassed the 100-million mark among people of Chinese descent worldwide. Like most Chinese parents, the Lees placed a heavy emphasis on their children's education. Lee Senior, a school principal, wanted his son to become a professor. However, the younger Lee's inclination was toward drama and the arts. For a Chinese, his career interest was unconventional. This was the 1970s. The children of middle-class Chinese families were expected to pursue a respectable occupation that had good prospects and provide security to the family. Rather unimaginative and predictable, they would want their children to follow the well-trodden path of becoming professionals, business people, and scholars.

Following the completion of his military service in his country at age twenty-five, the young Lee enrolled for a course in theater at the University of Illinois at Urbana-Champaign in 1979. Upon finishing, he pursued his master's of fine arts in the Tisch School of the Arts at New York University. Coincidentally, the Taiwanese was a classmate of the future American director, producer, writer, and actor Spike Lee, who, despite sharing the same surname, has no known blood relationship with him. In fact, the two Lees worked together on a thesis film. Both men would later create works that reflect their ethnic heritage. Lee's talent was apparent even while he was doing his master's. His short film entitled *Shades of the Lake* in 1982 won the Best Drama Award in Short Film in Taiwan. A drama called *The Fine Line*, which he made as his graduate thesis in 1984, won him the New York University's Wasserman Award for Outstanding Direction.

After graduation, the aspiring screenplay writer and director found few opportunities. The reality was that vacancies for screenplay writers and movie directors were always few and far between. Furthermore, the global audience of the early 1980s showed little interest in authentic Asian films by Asian directors. Although he made little progress career-wise for years, Lee persevered with his dream of creating films and explored new ideas for his screenplays.

In 1990, Lee submitted two screenplays in a competition sponsored by Taiwan's Government Information Office. His *Pushing*

Hands and *The Wedding Banquet* took the top two places. It was this event that signaled the change in his luck and brought about the beginning of his career. The winning screenplays caught the attention of Li-Kong Hsu, a budding producer. The trouble with the arts is the incredibly subjective nature of its assessment. Beauty is indeed in the eyes of the beholder, and fortunately Hsu was attracted to Lee's eccentric style. Lee was invited to direct *Pushing Hands* as a full-length feature film. *Pushing Hands*, the first movie Lee directed, debuted in 1992. The story was about a tai chi instructor who emigrated from China to live with his son and American daughter-in-law in New York and the culture shock he encountered in his new environment. The interaction between changes brought about by modernity and Western values on the one hand and centuries-old Chinese traditions on the other would be a recurring theme of Lee's movies.

Pushing Hands became a success in the Taiwanese box office and received attention from the critics. The wide acclaim was reflected in the film's eight nominations at Taiwan's Golden Horse Film Festival. Not bad at all for a director's first attempt. Their successful collaboration spurred Hsu to invite Lee to direct another movie. The second film, *The Wedding Banquet*, which was released in 1993, was about a Taiwanese man living happily in a gay relationship in Manhattan without the knowledge of his traditional-minded parents back home. In an attempt to please his parents, who were eager to see him marry, he tied the knot with a woman from China. The drama gets interesting as his parents come to the United States to plan a grand wedding for him. It won eleven awards, including the Golden Bear in the Berlin Film Festival. In 1995, Lee's third film, *Eat Drink Man Woman*, which was about family conflicts in modern Taiwan, became a box office hit and received critical acclaim yet again. The film received the Best Foreign Language Film nomination in both the Golden Globe and Academy Awards for a second consecutive year and won five awards in total. Thus far, Lee's works have been Chinese-language films.

A breakthrough came in 1995 when Lee directed the British drama movie *Sense and Sensibility*, based on a Jane Austen novel. The star-studded cast included Emma Thompson, Kate Winslett, Hugh Grant, and Hugh Laurie. It was this English-language movie that gave Lee serious recognition internationally. The martial-arts themed *Crouching Tiger, Hidden Dragon* followed in 2000. This movie, featuring an international cast of famous Chinese actors from Hong Kong, Malaysia, China, and Taiwan, resulted in Lee's being nominated for an Academy Award for Best Director. In 2005, *Brokeback Mountain*, the controversial drama about a romantic relationship between two men in rural Wyoming, was released in cinemas. Lee won the Academy Award and the Golden Globe Award, both for Best Director. *Brokeback Mountain* also won the Golden Lion award for best film at the Venice International Film Festival, as well as awards for best film from the 2005 Broadcast Film Critics Association, Directors Guild of America, Writers Guild of America (Adapted Screenplay), Producers Guild of America, and the Independent Spirit Awards. Critics from all over the world, including Los Angeles, New York, Boston, and London, proclaimed it as 2005's best film. At the 2006 British Academy Awards (BAFTA), *Brokeback Mountain* won both the Best Film and Best Director awards. In total, the film received an amazing eight Academy Award nominations. Lee made history as the first Asian and non-Caucasian to win an Academy Award for Best Director. In 2007, Lee's film *Lust, Caution* earned him a second Golden Lion, making him one of only two directors to have ever won Venice's Golden Lion twice.

Today, Ang Lee is one of the world's most famous directors. Without full-time work for many years, Lee pursued a career in films even though he made no progress when he was well into his thirties. His story of being unemployed to becoming a huge success is remarkable. There is no denying that anyone in Lee's shoes must have had substantial strength of character to persevere when there was hardly a cloud with a silver lining on the horizon. These must come a point in the minds of every aspiring writer, singer, artist, or director when they doubt whether their efforts will eventually amount to anything at all after sacrificing so much. Are they really that good?

But many great achievers did not make it by themselves. Talent and perseverance can only take you so far. Opportunities and time for talent to develop must have been present. Who was the person instrumental in his success? It was none other than his wife and the mother of his two children, Jane Lin. While he wrote screenplays, Lin was the breadwinner. When asked in interview how he conceived the ideas for his films, Lee is said to have responded: "I don't find my films; my films find me." The years when Lee did not hold a job were crucial for him in making it as a director. It afforded him the time to explore various themes and plots with his creativity and for the ideas for his films to "find" him. During this period, he honed his craft and perfected his screenplays. *Pushing Hands* and *The Wedding Banquet*, the two of his works that essentially gave him that big break, were the result. It allowed him to search for opportunities. And his opportunity came with the competition organized by Taiwan's Government Information Office.

It is not difficult to imagine what immense pressure the Lees must have faced as a couple. In Chinese culture, it would have been extremely embarrassing for the woman to support her husband and the family. It takes a spouse with a great deal of faith to refrain from telling her husband after a couple of years to snap out of his dream and find a real job to help pay the bills. Would all his efforts be worth it? His breakthrough only came at age thirty-seven, when many men would have already reached the pinnacle of their careers. Thus, it is Lin's support for her husband that gave us *Sense and Sensibility, Crouching Tiger Hidden Dragon,* and *Brokeback Mountain.*

While Ang Lee was busy writing his screenplays, another no less inspiring story was in the making in another corner of the world. Joanne Rowling was born on July 31, 1965, in Yate, a quiet English town in Gloucestershire. Rowling discovered her passion for writing fantasy stories as a young child. The story goes that the publishers requested that her initials rather than her name be used out of concern that the target audience would not read her book if they knew that the author was a woman. Thus, in June 1997, the first book by J.K. Rowling was published. Within months, the book received prizes and awards. The first-time author won the Smarties Book Prize, the British Book Award for Children's Book of the Year, and the Children's Book Award. In July 1998, its sequel, *Harry Potter and the Chamber of Secrets,* was released. The third novel, *Harry Potter and the Prisoner of Azkaban,* followed in December 1999, winning the Whitbread

Children's Book of the Year Award in 2000. Rowling also won the Smarties Prize for the third time consecutively, making her the first person to do so. On July 8, 2000, Rowling's fourth book, *Harry Potter and the Goblet of Fire*, hit the bookstores in the United Kingdom and the United State simultaneously. On the first day, 372,775 copies of the book were sold in the United Kingdom, and another three million copies were sold in the first forty-eight hours in the United States. This was a sales record. The 2000 British Book Awards named Rowling author of the year. After an interval of a few years, the fifth installment of the Harry Potter series, *Harry and the Order of the Phoenix*, was published in 2003. On July 16, 2005, the sixth book, *Harry Potter and the Half-Blood Prince*, was released. Selling nine million copes in the first twenty-four hours, it broke all previous sales records. Yet *Harry Potter and the Deathly Hallows,* released on July 21, 2007, managed to smash its predecessor's record as the fastest-selling book of all time when eleven million copies were purchased on the first day in the United Kingdom and the United States.

Within the span of a decade, Rowling became one of the most successful authors in history. Four of her books have consecutively set records as the fastest selling ever. In total, the Harry Potter series, which has been translated into more than sixty-five languages, had collectively sold more than 400 million copies by June 2008. In 2010, *Forbes* named Rowling as one of the richest women in the world and estimated her wealth to be worth US$1 billion. She received the Order of the British Empire (OBE) in 2000 and was presented the Legion of Honour by French President Nicolas Sarkozy in 2009. She was also awarded a string of honorary degrees from St. Andrews University, University of Edinburgh, Napier University, University of Exeter, and

Harvard University. In 2010, Rowling won the inaugural Hans Christian Andersen Literature Award, which was established in honor of the legendary Danish author.

Rowling's remarkable journey from rags to riches is truly the stuff of fairytales. From an unemployed single mother completing her first book on an old typewriter, she became a multi-millionaire. Overcoming overwhelming odds, she rose from obscurity to one of the most famous names in the literary world. Legend has it that Rowling looked at the list of literary agents in a public library and chose Christopher Little, a small literary agency, as it sounded like a character from a children's book. From the very beginning, the odds were against Rowling. The manuscript that she sent went straight into the reject basket. Little was of the view that children's books have little potential. However, the unusual black binding caught the eye of Bryony Evens, his office manager at that time. This prompted Evens to read the synopsis. Evens showed it to Little, and the Christopher Little Literary Agents agreed to represent Rowling in finding a publisher. Twelve publishing houses rejected Rowling's book. Finally, Bloomsbury, a small London-based publisher, accepted Rowling's manuscript. Apparently, the credit for the decision to publish Rowling's book goes to Alice Newton, the eight-year-old daughter of Bloomsbury's chairman, who was given the first chapter to review by her father. Nevertheless, Bloomsbury's skepticism of the book's success was evident. Rowling was given a small advance of fifteen hundred British pounds. She was further advised to have a proper career as it was doubtful that there was a real possibility that her book would make money. In June 1997, Bloomsbury published *Philosopher's Stone*. The initial print run produced only one thousand copies, and, even so, half of them were distributed to libraries. Today, these first copies are valued between sixteen thousand and twenty-five thousand British pounds.

The Harry Potter series magically transformed Bloomsbury from a small publishing house to a constituent of the FTSE SmallCap Index, the index of small market capitalization companies listed on the London Stock Exchange. In 1995, Bloomsbury was floated as a public registered company, and Bloomsbury USA was established in 1998. In 1999 and 2000, the British Book Industry named the company Publisher of the Year.

How did Rowling become successful? She has famously said that the plot in Harry Potter "strolled into her head fully formed" in 1990 while on a train from Manchester to London. By the time the train arrived at King's Cross station, not only had Rowling came upon the idea of a young boy attending a school of wizardry but many of the story's characters have been conceived as well. She began to write immediately as soon as she got back to her London flat. So why did it take seven years for her first book to be published? Rowling wrote during her lunch breaks while she worked at Amnesty International. However, it was only in 1995, when she was unemployed, that she was able to seriously engage in writing and completing the book. Readers assume that once their favorite authors have the plots in their heads, they are able to churn out pages profusely. One would presume that these larger-than-life authors effortlessly put their thoughts onto paper and are not faced with writer's block, like we are. Every sentence that comes forth from the pen of a great writer is perfect and immaculate. After all, they are literary geniuses. The reality, however, is somewhat different.

Writing involves a great deal of time and concentration. A person holding a full-time job would be spending no less than eight hours at work and another hour or two commuting to and from the office. The rest of their waking hours would be spent on meals, buying groceries, performing household chores, attending to personal and family matters, or simply preparing for or unwinding from work. Whatever time available after a long, tiring, and hectic day is spent vegetating on the couch in front of the television or reading a favorite book. An author needs time to write, review, reflect, rewrite, and refine. Even when Rowling created her fourth novel, the seasoned writer admitted that she rewrote one chapter thirteen times. Imagine how much effort Rowling would have to put into just one book. While Rowling's meteoric rise despite her bleak start is another inspiring story for a motivational book, her story has been sensationalized. Rowling was not unemployable. She graduated with a degree from the University of Exeter, a top British university. When Rowling was completing her first book in 1995, she was a single mother of a two-year-old child. It must have been a tremendous challenge attempting to complete her book and caring for a toddler, who would have required from her a very substantial amount of time. Thus, Rowling chose to be without a job. Like Ang Lee, she needed the time to discover the full potential of her creativity.

Consider the plot of the TV series "Supernatural." Sam and Dean Winchester, two brothers from Kansas, make it their full-time jobs to travel around the whole length of the United States hunting and vanquishing ghosts, demons, and a host of other supernatural beings. Strangely, no explanation is given as to where they get money to pay for food, fuel, motel accommodation, and Dean's occasional visits to the strip clubs. That may be expected of Hollywood movies, but in the real world, bills for a variety of expenses need to be paid. So if van Gogh could not make a living from selling his art, what was his source of income? While he received no monetary aid from his cash-strapped church minister father, the unfailing financial support from Theo, his art dealer younger brother, allowed Vincent van Gogh to fully focus his work. Although he started painting only in his late twenties, being a full-time artist allowed him to be prolific. Without his brother, it would have been impossible for van Gogh to leave behind nine hundred paintings as well as eleven hundred drawings and sketches. We see the work of geniuses but often take for granted how much time and effort is required by all geniuses to achieve the end result.

Often overlooked in the van Gogh story is how he became an artist. In 1869, his Uncle Cent assisted in getting him hired as an art dealer in Goupil & Cie in The Hague. Goupil & Cie was a leading international art dealership with offices also in Paris, London, Brussels, Berlin, Vienna, and New York. In 1873, he was seconded to Goupil & Co. in London. It was during his years spent with the firm that van Gogh was exposed to the works of master artists. By studying art, van Gogh found his true calling. Fortunately, Uncle Cent was in the art dealership business. This was the 1800s. There were no career fairs, student counselors, or employment agencies. It was still an era when many young men took up a trade by way of apprenticeship with their fathers or close family members rather than responding to a job advertisement. Had Uncle Cent been a candle maker, van Gogh's destiny would have been to melt wax into molds.

Coming back to Thomas Edison, his background had all the trappings of an inspiring story. He was one of seven children born to parents of humble means, and there was a time in his life when he had to sell candy, newspapers, and vegetables. However, he had two lucky breaks that would put him on the path to become an inventor. The first was that he obtained a job as a telegraph operator from a man whose son he saved from being run over by a train. The science behind this new technology intrigued him. This can be seen in some of his earliest inventions that were related to telegraphy. The second was that Edison had the amazingly good fortune of being acquainted to Frank Leonard Pope, a fellow telegrapher. Pope, an inventor himself who also played a significant role in the technological advances of the nineteenth century, became not only Edison's mentor in his early years but allowed Edison, a struggling young man at that time, to live and work in the basement of his home. Pope and Edison became partners and invented a one-wire telegraph in 1870. Although their partnership did not last long, it allowed Edison to be acquainted with this technology and establish himself as an inventor. After Edison sold his invention, the quadruplex telegraph, to Western Union for ten thousand dollars, he had the funds to build the first industrial research laboratory in history in Menlo Park, New Jersey. By the time he conducted the experiment that would lead to the invention of the light bulb, he was a full-time inventor with sufficient finances, his own laboratory, and a dedicated team of researchers. Edison was not only an inventor but also an entrepreneur. He formed a number of companies, including General Electric, one of the largest publicly traded companies in the world. Edison was able to capitalize on his inventions, and the profits he made enabled him to fund the research toward other inventions. How else would Edison have found the time and resources to make hundreds or even thousands of attempts to discover what does or doesn't work? Each try would have taken hours. It is undeniable that perseverance is an essential ingredient for success. But perseverance requires time. And time is money.

Ang Lee had his wife. Vincent van Gogh had his brother, and Edison had Pope until he found his own footing. Like everyone else, Rowling, too, needed both time and money. It was the financial support from the British welfare system that made it happen. In Britain, the Liberal government of Henry Campbell-Bannerman laid the foundation of its modern welfare system. The British social welfare system has not only alleviated the least fortunate from poverty by providing them income and homes but has also played a vital role in giving opportunities to budding but penniless artists, writers, and musicians to succeed.

Behind every inspirational story is an untold story. The truth is that no matter how remarkably brilliant or exceptionally talented you are, you can never do it alone.

CHAPTER 4:
LUCKY BREAK

The year was 1566. The restless forces of the mighty Ottoman Empire were on the march again. This time their quest was to capture Vienna, which lay just beyond the northern border of their immense empire. Assembled for this enterprise was a massive army of 100,000 men, an enormous number by the standards of the day. Leading this seemingly endless column of soldiers and camp followers was Suleiman the Magnificient himself. The Ottomans had previously tried to conquer the seat of power of the Habsburg Empire in 1529. Unable to breach the walls, the Turks were finally forced to abandon the siege due to unusually heavy snowfall, as if by divine intervention. The withdrawal ended in disaster. Baggage and artillery were lost as a result of the extreme weather conditions. In addition, the retreating troops were ambushed in western Slovakia. Now, at age seventy-one, the frail sultan returned with a vengeance to make one final attempt at taking Austria's capital. As the largest and most powerful sovereign state in Western Christendom, the Habsburg Empire was the only formidable foe standing in the way of the total domination of the continent by the zealous Muslim warriors. However, fate had it that Suleiman would not have the opportunity to catch a glimpse of this historic city along the Danube River again. In the line of advance of the Ottomans was Szigetvar Fortress in Hungary. From August 5 to September 8, a twenty-three-hundred-man detachment of the Habsburg army comprising ethnic Croats and Hungarians made a heroic stand and fought to the death in the siege of Szigetvar.

The battle could only have one outcome. Overwhelming numbers ensured an Ottoman victory, and the garrison under their aristocratic commander, Nicholas Zrinsky, was annihilated. However, more than twenty thousand Turks lost their lives. Although the road to Vienna now lay open, the Ottomans unfortunately would not be following up on their victory. A day before the battle ended, the caliph of Islam had died in his tent of natural causes. Europe was saved yet again with the withdrawal of the sultan's troops, as it was the custom to settle the important question of succession to the throne. It was not until 1683 that the persistent Turks returned.

Among the world empires, the story of the Ottomans is probably the most remarkable. In the early sixteenth century, it was already one of the most powerful political entities on earth. Ottoman troops were stationed as far as the sandy beaches of Goa, fighting in support of local Indian Muslims against the newly arrived Portuguese explorers. Selim I, Suleiman's father, had expanded the empire's boundaries by conquering Egypt and defeating the Persians at the Battle of Chaldiran. The important Muslim cities of Mecca, Medina, Jerusalem, Damascus, and Baghdad were part of the Ottoman realm. Upon becoming sultan in 1520, Suleiman captured Belgrade in 1521 and conquered Hungary following his victory at the Battle of Mohacs in 1526. The Balkan states had fallen like dominoes to his armies, and Europe could have been subjugated if they were not stopped at Vienna. Large parts of North Africa as far as modern-day Algeria were incorporated into his domain. The Ottoman navy dominated the Mediterranean Sea and even had a formidable presence in the Red Sea and the Persian Gulf. Barbary corsairs owing allegiance to the Ottoman sultan were raiding as far north as Iceland for blond Nordic slaves. By the end of his reign, Suleiman had approximately fifteen million subjects.

The Ottoman Empire at its greatest extent in the sixteenth and seventeenth centuries spanned three continents. It consisted of twenty-nine provinces and numerous vassal states, effectively controlling much of the Middle East, North Africa, and Southeastern Europe. Its sphere of influence extended east as far as what is now Indonesia, when the sultanate of Aceh on the island of Sumatera declared itself an Ottoman vassal in 1565. In the stormy Atlantic Ocean, Lanzarote in the Canary Islands was captured in 1585. The Ottomans were once merely a miniscule Turkic tribe originally from Central Asia. Popular folklore has it that the founder of the dynasty, Osman I, led a band of 444 warriors. How could a tiny and inconspicuous band of nomads come to rule huge swathes of the world?

Ascending the throne to reap the fruits of Suleiman's empire-building was Selim II, his son by the legendary beauty Roxelana. Known by the Turkish name Hurrem, Roxelana was one of many thousands of European girls forcibly taken from their homelands over the centuries and selected for their good looks to become concubines of the Ottoman sultans. In his harem, there must have been a bevy of gorgeous women, but Suleiman fell head over heels for Roxelana. Although a strong ruler, the Commander of the Faithful's infatuation for the Slavic maiden allowed her to have an immense influence on him and his decisions. Intelligent and ambitious, she regularly intervened in foreign affairs, including engineering an alliance between the Ottoman Empire and the Kingdom of Poland. Her letters to the Polish King Sigismund II Augustus, which have been preserved to this day, are a testament of this fact. It was Roxelana's sway at Suleiman's court that ensured that her son became the next sultan. However, Selim proved to be a weak ruler, and it was Sokollu Mehmed Paşa, the grand vizier, who held de facto power.

An able and competent statesman, Mehmed continued to expand the borders of the Ottoman Empire. European states along its borders such as Transylvania, Wallachia, and Moldavia were compelled by Mehmed to pay tribute. In 1568, Mehmed concluded a treaty with Emperor Maximillian II whereby even the Habsburgs would pay a yearly tribute. To the south, Hejaz and Yemen in the Arabian peninsular were conquered. After the crushing and humiliating defeat of the Ottomans at the naval Battle of Lepanto in 1571 by a coalition of European Christian nations, the dynamic and insightful Mehmed oversaw the quick rebuilding of a massive Ottoman fleet. The result was that, within a year, the Ottomans once again had one of the largest navies and some of the biggest ships in the Mediterranean. The grand vizier did not forget his Christian relatives and ensured their advancement. Mehmed made his brother, Makarije, the patriach of Pec, a prominent position in the Serbian Orthodox Church. His nephew Antonije Sokolovic was first installed as the archbishop of Ochryd and shortly thereafter the patriach of Pec. When Antonije died, Gerasim Sokolovic, another of Mehmed's nephews, took over the office.

As the most powerful man in the Ottoman Empire other than the sultan himself, Mehmed became one of the empire's richest persons. At his peak, he was estimated to be worth eighteen million ducats. As a testament of his wealth, power, and influence, Mehmed commissioned the construction of numerous remarkable buildings renowned for their architecture. In Istanbul, they include the Sokollu

Mehmed Pasa Mosque, Sokollu Mehmed Turbe, the Azapkapi Mosque, Sokollu Mehmed Pasa Kulliyesi, which includes a school and his tomb, and the Sokollu Mehmed Pasa Complex, which consists of a caravanserai, bathhouse, mosque, school, market streets, and private apartments. Many other complexes, bridges, and public bathhouses throughout the empire were also built in his name. All these buildings and structures were designed by Mimar Sinan, one of history's most famous architects.

Until his assassination in 1579, Sokollu Mehmed Pasa became ruler of the mighty Ottoman Empire in all but name. Who exactly was this man? Mehmed, Mimar Sinan, Roxelana, and so many of the characters that played a pivotal role in contributing to the greatness of this Muslim empire had one thing in common. They all came from Christian families of humble means living in the Ottoman Empire or just outside its borders and were selected because of their talents, abilities, good looks, or some other desirable attributes.

As Sokollu Mehmed Pasa only received the attention of historians after he became prominent, the exact details of his background are unclear. What is certain is that he was of Serbian origin and brought up as an Orthodox Christian. It is believed that he came from a family of shepherds living near the town of Sokolovici and was taken by Ottoman officials in 1516. Named after the prophet, Mehmed was trained as a Janissary and distinguished himself in the great Battle of Mohacs and the assault on Vienna in 1529. His abilities allowed him to quickly rise through the ranks, becoming in quick succession the commander of the Imperial Guard, high admiral of the fleet, governor of the province of Rumelia, and, ultimately, the grand vizier for three sultans.

Mimar Sinan, the chief architect of Suleyman the Magnificient and a favorite of Mehmed, was born to a Christian stonemason in a small town in Anatolia. In 1512, he was conscripted into the Janissary Corps under the devshirme system. His talents and intellectual qualities came to the attention of state officials, and he was assigned as an apprentice to leading architects. Sinan took part in a number of important military campaigns, where he proved himself both as an able engineer and architect. Other than the buildings and structures commissioned by Sokullu Mehmed Pasa, Suleymaniye Mosque, Selimiye Mosque, Mihrimah Sultan Mosque, Sehzade Mosque, and Banya Bashi Mosque are among his legacy.

Roxelana, the daughter of an Orthodox priest, hailed from a part of Ukraine that was at that time part of the Kingdom of Poland. Carried off in a raid by Muslim Crimean Tartars, the attractive buxom brunette became the mother of six of the sultan's children. Had she not been abducted and forced into the harem of the Sultan of Sultans, she would have most certainly lived an insignificant life and died a commoner. Instead she negotiated and concluded an alliance with the Polish king.

At Adrianople (1365), Kosovo (1389), Varna (1444), Constantinople (1453), Mohacs (1526), and countless other battles, the Christian European nations were decisively defeated at the hands of the Turks. The Ottomans did not have any secret weapons, and both the Europeans and the Turks shared the same technology in warfare. What made the Ottoman army victorious time and again? The answer lies within the ranks of the Ottoman army. Numbering tens of thousands, special troops called Janissaries were both respected and feared by their foes. As the vanguard of the Turkish threat to Europe, even today the Janissary has remained one of the potent symbols of Islam in the European psyche. But what made the Janissaries so formidable? And how were they different from the soldiers of Christian Europe?

Firstly, the Janissaries were professional soldiers in the employment of the state. Like the officers and enlisted men of today's armies, they received regular salaries and were subjected to intense military training even in times of peace. Thus, the Ottomans had the first standing army to march in the battlegrounds of Europe since the era of the Roman Empire. Unsurprisingly, the Janissaries are often compared to the elite Roman Praetorian Guard. Unfortunately for the Christian nations of Europe, they had no equivalent. Instead, kings depended on feudal lords to fulfill their obligations to raise troops only when war was looming. The conventional practice of that era was that other than a small retinue of retainers and men-at-arms, the vast majority of soldiers were hastily recruited, armed, and provisioned by the nobility only in times of hostilities. Although the crusading knights such as the Hospitallers, Templars, Teutonic Knights, and other military monastic orders have often been compared to the Janissaries, they were far fewer in number and did not owe their allegiance to any particular European state.

Secondly, the intense training of the Janissaries produced among the best soldiers. Even one of the greatest military leaders who fought the Ottoman forces was himself a former Janissary. Gjergi Kastrioti, Albania's national hero, began his military career with the Ottoman army. In 1443, while fighting against the Hungarians led by John Hunyandi, he deserted and returned to his homeland with a contingent of Janissaries of Albanian origin. Reaffirming the Christian faith of his birth, he led the resistance to the Turks and destroyed the garrison of Kruja. His military skills presented a major obstacle to the expansion of his former masters. Between 1443 and 1468, he defeated five armies sent against him. This nemesis of the Ottomans is better known as Skanderbeg or Iskandar Bey, his given Muslim name. The successful campaigns of Skanderbeg and, to a lesser extent, Vlad Tepes have been credited by historians with stalling the advancement of the Turks, giving time for the Christian nations to prepare. Vlad Tepes, who is revered by some and detested by others, was taken as a hostage by the Ottomans. In addition to learning the Quran and the Turkish language, he, too, received the military training of the Janissaries. While his brother Radu remained a Muslim and served as a commander of a Janissary contingent, Vlad Tepes returned to his native Wallachia. Better known as Vlad the Impaler or Dracula, he led the Romanian resistance against the Turks. Like Skanderbeg, his success was attributed to the superb military skills he acquired through his training under the Ottomans.

Thirdly, in their battles with the Turks, the Christians encountered among their foes large numbers of men who were similar to them in physical appearance. The Turks were by this time ethnically diverse and highly inclusive of conquered peoples. Converts were welcomed into their fold. A European becomes a Turk upon embracing Islam and faces no discrimination whatsoever. The Janissaries were recruited solely from European Christian youths, who were then required to become Muslims. As such, like the earliest followers of the Prophet who burst forth from Arabia to conquer the Middle East and North Africa and the Berbers who overran Spain in the seventh century, the Janissaries fought with the fiery fervor of converts when engaging their infidel enemies.

Finally, perhaps the most significant success factor was that the Janissaries were not only chosen but were promoted based entirely on meritocracy. How did the devshirme system come about? In the fifteenth century, the Turkish Candarli family had been so powerful and influential that five of their members became grand viziers. The last of them, Candarli Halil Pasha, even deposed and replaced an Ottoman sultan. In 1453, after the fall of Constantinople, Mehmet II, the reigning sultan, had Candarli Halil Pasha executed and his property confiscated. The lesson, however, was not lost. The influence of the Turkic tribal chieftains must be severely curtailed. With Candarli Halil Pasha's bloody end, there began the emergence of a new and separate class of officials and administrators who had no ties to any tribe or community but owed absolute allegiance to his majesty. The mechanism to achieve this purpose was the devshirme system. In 1456, Veli Mahmud Pasa or Mahmud Pasha Angelovic, an Ottoman general from a Christian Serbo-Croatian background, took office as grand vizier, and other graduates of the devshirme system quickly followed suit. The prevailing view among Muslim jurists was that Islam does not allow the enslavement of fellow Muslims. Thus, this highly unpopular practice involved the forced removal of boys from Christian families for service in the Ottoman administration. State officials, many of whom were themselves recruited under the devshirme system, scoured Christian villages and towns in the Balkans in search of the brightest, strongest, and most talented boys between the ages of ten and twelve. Upon enrollment, they would be subjected to strict discipline and were given the best training afforded in the empire. An assessment would be made based on their talents and natural abilities for selection to serve in one of the four state institutions, namely the palace, the scribes, the ulema, or religious institution and the military. The brightest were handpicked for the Palace. Those who proved their capability quickly moved up the ranks.

The forced conscription must have caused untold pain and sorrow for the Christians. Ties to their families were severed. Parents who feared the loss of their sons reviled the devshirme system. This was an age when religion was still foremost above all else. For the many parents who were faithful to their religion, they would be concerned that the souls of their sons would be damned for eternity as a result of abjuring their faith. In many cases, desperate Christian parents resorted to bribing officials and hiding their sons.

However, for the brightest and most able young men, the opportunities offered were almost limitless. As their career advancement was entirely merit based, social background and ethnicity were no impediments. The only requirement was becoming a Muslim. The best of the best could aspire to the highest office of the empire other than that of the sultan himself. Between the fifteenth and seventeenth centuries, most of the grand viziers, the incredibly powerful chief ministers, came through the devshirme system. Cigalazade Yusuf Sinan Pasha was of Italian background. Born in Messina, Sicily, he was captured at the Battle of Djerba by the

Ottoman navy in 1560. He held many high positions in the empire, including an agha of the Janissaries and the high admiral of the Ottoman fleet. Cigalazade took part in many successful campaigns, including the wars against the Persians, and was instrumental in the notable victory at the Battle of Mezo-Keresztes. He eventually married two granddaughters of Suleyman the Magnificient. Hadim Sinan Pasha, the favorite grand vizier of Selim I, was a Bosnian who distinguished himself fighting the Persians in the Battle of Chaldiran and defeating the Mamelukes at Khan Yunis. These offspring of infidels effectively controlled all aspects of the Ottoman Empire.

Over the centuries, hundreds of thousands of Balkan children fought as Janissaries. They were the creme de la creme of the Albanian, Greek, Serb, Croat, Bulgarian, and Bosnian boys of that era. Even Georgians, Italians, Poles, Ukrainians, and Russians who were taken captive during raids outside of the empire's borders were enlisted. Aside from the devshirme, there was another institution affiliated with the Ottoman Empire that provided similar opportunities for advancement to capable Christian young men of humble origins: the Barbary corsairs.

In 1565, one of the most decisive battles between Christians and Muslims took place in the Mediterranean. Among the many distinguished Ottoman naval commanders who participated in the famous Great Siege of Malta was Uluj Ali. When the great admiral Turgut Reis died during the siege, he was made Turgut's successor by Piyale Pasha. Uluj Ali was born Giovanni Dionigi Galeni in a village in Calabria, Southern Italy. In 1536, the young Italian was captured by the corsair fleet of Barbarossa Hayreddin Pasha and became a galley slave. Eventually, he joined the corsairs, many of whom, like him, were forcibly taken in raids on Christian lands and subsequently became Muslims. His remarkable abilities as a mariner allowed him to rise rapidly within the ranks. He eventually became a captain of a galley and made a reputation as one of the boldest corsairs in the Mediterranean. He sailed with Turgut Reis, the Ottoman admiral and bey of Tripoli. Due to his success in battles, Uluj Ali became governor of Alexandria. Turgut himself was captured from a Christian village along the Aegean coast by corsairs during his youth. Handpicked for his extraordinary talent in handling weapons, he was given intensive training and became an outstanding gunner. It was his ability to use siege artillery with deadly effect that catapulted him to success and earned him fame as a superb naval commander. Turgut first saw action in Egypt and served in the fleet of Sinan Reis. He soon had a remarkable track record of scoring hits on enemy ships with his cannons. By 1520, Turgut was serving in the fleet of the legendary Barbarossa Hayreddin Pasha, born to the widow of a Greek Orthodox priest. Turgut soon became Barbarossa's chief lieutenant and commanded twelve vessels. Their fleet wreaked havoc on the coasts of the Mediterranean, enslaving many thousands of Europeans. When Barbarossa died in 1546, Turgut succeeded him as the supreme commander of the Ottoman naval forces in the Mediterranean.

Some of those carried off by the Barbary corsairs were destined for even greater things. Pargali Ibrahim Pasha, the grand vizier who preceded Sokollu Mehmed Pasa, was the son of a Christian sailor from Epirus, Greece. Not only did he become the grand vizier, he even married Sultan Suleyman's sister. Thus, the son of a commoner became the brother-in-law of one of the mightiest rulers on the planet.

Ibrahim's magnificent palace in Istanbul has been transformed into the Turkish and Islamic Arts Museum.

In the 1995 film *Bravehart*, Mel Gibson portrays William Wallace, the hero of Scottish resistance against the English invaders, as a common peasant who sought vengeance for the unjust execution of his wife. The historical Sir William Wallace, however, was a nobleman who held lands throughout Scotland. Similarly, while the Balian portrayed by Orlando Bloom in the 2005 film *Kingdom of Heaven* was a poor blacksmith in a remote village in France, the real Balian of Ibelin was a prominent nobleman. It was probably the intention of the film directors to allow moviegoers to connect with the protagonists of their fictionalized versions of these historical epics.

Throughout the centuries, the European armies were almost exclusively led by the noblest of aristocrats. John Hunyadi, the iconic nemesis of the Ottomans in the mid-fifteenth century, was from a powerful aristocratic family. Hunyadi was the voivode of Transylvania and his son, Matthias Corvinus, became the king of Hungary. The Christian naval coalition, which decisively defeated the Ottoman fleet in the 1571 Battle of Lepanto, was commanded by Don Juan of Austria, the son of the Holy Roman Emperor Charles V and half-brother of King Philip of Spain. When Hayreddin Barbarossa defeated the combined fleet of the Christian states in the Battle of Preveza, his archenemy, the imperial admiral Andrea Doria, also came from one of the noblest and most ancient of Genoese ruling families.

In the Great Siege of Malta of 1565, the military opponent of Piyale Pasha, Turgut Reis, and Uluj Ali was Jean Parisot de la Valette, the grand master of the Knights Hospitallers. As supreme commander of the Christian defenders of Malta, he is forever immortalized in history by repelling the numerically superior Turks against overwhelming odds, and the capital of Malta is named in his memory. Parisot was the scion of one of the noblest families in France. For many generations, his ancestors have fought beside the kings of France, including during the First, Second, Fourth, Fifth, and Sixth Crusades. Jean Parisot's grandfather was a king's ordely, and his father was a chevalier de France. In the 1683 siege of Vienna, when the Turks were decisively beaten, the Christian coalition forces were led by Ernst Rudiger, the count of Starhemberg, and John III Sobieski, the king of Poland. Prince Eugene of Savoy, who successfully led the Austrians in their military campaigns against the Turks in the 1700s, came from an aristocratic Savoyard family.

It goes without saying that the commander of any army plays a pivotal role in winning or losing a battle. Evidently, the brilliance of Alexander the Great was crucial in the many Greek victories. However, Alexander himself would certainly not have had the opportunity to command the Macedonian army and implement his winning strategies had he not been king. Until modern times, European armies were led by the noblest or aristocrats. It would be the king himself if he was present, otherwise the highest ranking of the lords. While the Macedonians were fortunate to have a military genius in Alexander, the incompetent Guy of Lusignan caused the downfall of his Kingdom of Jerusalem when he led a powerful army to certain destruction at the Horns of Hattin. In 1396, Phillip of Eu, count of Artois and constable of France, foolishly led a charge at the Battle of Nicopolis that handed the victory to the Turks over a mighty coalition of Hungarian, Wallachian,

German, French, Burgundian, and troops of many nationalities. The fate of a soldier in a medieval European army depended on the capability and intelligence of his aristocratic commander.

On the one hand, we have the European armies where a tiny pool of men of noble birth was given the privilege to command. On the other hand, we have the Ottomans, who have systematically picked the best man from throughout their empire and trained him for the job. Born to peasants, shepherds, fishermen, and others of humble means, they would have otherwise been destined to live out lives of obscurity and insignificance. Undeniably for these youngsters in the devshirme, it must have been an extremely daunting experience as they were permanently separated from everyone and everything they knew. Overnight, they were placed in an alien environment with men barking orders at them in a foreign tongue and compelled to embrace a strange faith detested by their families. Yet this was the only avenue available for a talented Christian peasant boy to move up in life. Had they served in the ranks of the Christian European armies, their socio-economic background would have relegated them to merely foot soldiers. For Mehmed Sokollu Pasa, Mimar Sinan, Roxelana, and countless others, their incorporation into the Ottoman system was an intervention that changed their destinies. In hindsight, the Ottoman recruiters were like the "American Idol" judges who scoured the country for the best talent. For the chosen ones, it was the big break that transformed their lives and catapulted them to superstardom.

CHAPTER 5:
TO SURVIVE IS TO SUCCEED

It was Friday, May 14, 1948. The last of Britain's 100,000 troops stationed in Palestine headed home as the British Mandate came to an end. On that afternoon, a crowd waited in anticipation inside a small hall in the coastal city of Tel Aviv. At 4:00 p.m., David Ben-Gurion, the first prime minister of a fledgling nation, banged his wooden gavel, and everyone rose in unison to sing "Hatikva," the national anthem. Hundreds of people gathered outside the hall as tens of thousands more tuned in to the "Voice of Israel" to hear the station's first broadcast. When Ben-Gurion proclaimed the establishment of *Medinat Yisrael*, members of the audience rose to cheer and applaud. Many burst into tears.

One of those who added their signatures on the Declaration of Independence was a no-nonsense lady originally from Milwaukee, Wisconsin, who recalled in her memoirs:

"...My hands shook. We had done it. We had brought the Jewish people into existence... The long exile was over. Now we were a nation like other nations, masters—for the first time in twenty centuries—of our own destiny.

All I can recall about my actual signing of the proclamation is that I was crying openly, not able even to wipe the tears from my face... David Pincus asked me why I was crying and I said, 'One, because of the honor, and two, because there are people missing

E Ong

here...who had more of a right to be here and sign'... I wept almost beyond control."

That signatory, Golda Meir, the "Iron Lady" of Israeli politics, would eventually serve her country in the capacities of foreign minister and ultimately prime minister. Ten years before at the Evian Conference, Meir was said to have remarked to the press, "There is only one thing I hope to see before I die and that is that my people should not need expressions of sympathy anymore."

It was a day that had an immense impact on history. Palestinians call this event al Nakba or "the Catastrophe." The world is still deeply divided over the creation of the State of Israel, and whenever the topic is discussed, the conversation tends to get heated.

At 5:25 a.m. the following day, the first Egyptian bombs hit Tel Aviv as the Jews observed the Sabbath. The 1948 Arab-Israeli War had begun. The armies of Egypt, Syria, Jordan, Iraq, and Lebanon invaded a small strip of land at the eastern shore of the Mediterranean. They were joined by volunteer fighters from Morocco, Sudan, Yemen, and Saudi Arabia with the objective of annihilating the world's only Jewish majority state at its inception. Opposing the Arab armies were a number of armed Jewish paramilitary groups, the most important and largest of which was Hagana, the forerunner of the Israeli Defence Force. In their ranks were tens of thousands of immigrants from Europe. Most had no previous military training. Some came to realize Theodore Herzl's dream of having a homeland of their own after 1,878 years in exile. But many were simply traumatized refugees who had fled Hitler's Final Solution. Hailing from countries as diverse as Poland, Czechoslovakia, Hungary, Romania, Yugoslavia, Russia, and the Baltic nations, they were the survivors of the centuries-old Jewish communities that had been permanently obliterated. As many as six million of their relatives and neighbors perished in Auschwitz, Treblinka, and other death camps.

A number of notable people fought in what was to the Israelis the War of Independence. An author of several books, including *A Year of Beauty and Health,* is world-renowned celebrity hairstylist Vidal Sassoon. He was made famous for the chain of saloons in the United States and Britain and the 1970s TV series called "Your New Day with Vidal Sassoon." By the early 1980s, Procter & Gamble used his name for their shampoos and conditioners available worldwide. Sasson's father was from Thessaloniki, while his mother's family hailed from Kiev. Both cities were heavily Jewish at one time. A member of the 43 Group, a Jewish organization that broke up Fascist meetings in East London after the end of the World War II, he saw combat in the 1948 Arab-Israeli War. In 1982, Sassoon started the Vidal Sasson International Center for the Study of Antisemitism at the Hebrew University of Jerusalem, an interdisciplinary research center that gathers information about antisemitism. In the 2009 Birthday Honours, Sassoon was appointed Commander of the Order of the British Empire (CBE).

Another veteran of Israel's War of Independence is Frank Lowy. His family ran a grocery shop in a small rural town in Czechoslovakia. When the Nazis arrived, Lowy's family sought refuge in Budapest. When Germany invaded Hungary in 1944, he had to survive on the streets. There, he learned skills that he would find useful for the rest of his life. Lowy's father had disappeared when he tried to purchase train tickets for his wife and four children. After World War II, Lowy made his way to France and boarded the *Yagur,* where, together with 750 other Jewish immigrants, he headed for the British Mandate of Palestine. Enlisting at age seventeen, Lowy fought in the Golani Brigade, which today is one of the elite units of the Israeli army. In 1952, Lowy left for Australia to reunite with his surviving family members. Arriving penniless, Lowy had almost no knowledge of English and started working by delivering sandwiches in Sydney. Today, he is at the helm of a global shopping center empire. Together with John Saunders, a Hungarian Jewish holocaust survivor, Lowy founded the Westfield Group.

With corporate offices in Sydney, London, Los Angeles, and Auckland, the Westfield Group is among the largest retail property groups in the world by equity market capitalization. One of the largest entities listed on the Australian Securities Exchange shopping center groups, as of 2012, it has interests in more than 104 shopping centers in Australia, New Zealand, Britain, the United States, and Brazil. With assets valued at more than A$62.9 billion and employing four thousand employees worldwide, many of Westfield's shopping centers are located in prime commercial areas with major retailers as their long-term anchor tenants. Also prominent in the management of assets on behalf of investors, Westfield has been involved in joint ventures on specific properties with partners such as AMP Capital Investors, Australian Prime Property Fund (APPF), DEXUS Property Group, Forest City Enterprises, JP Morgan Asset Management Real Estate Investment Management, Morgan Stanley Real Estate Management, the Perron Group, and Prudential Plc. In 2010, according to *Business Review Weekly*, Lowy had amassed a fortune estimated at A$5.04 billion, making him the wealthiest person in Australia. Among his connections to Israel is the establishment of the Tel Aviv University-affiliated Institute for National Strategy and Policy. In an interview in 2010, Lowy disclosed that he only knew the fate of his father in 1991 by chance while in the United States. "The sense of loss was so great, it still traumatizes me now," says Lowy. His father was beaten to death at Auschwitz when he insisted on retrieving the bag containing his prayer shawl that the guards took from him.

Wherever they went, they thrived. In 2004, the University of Hong Kong presented the award of an honorary doctorate of laws to one of Asia's most prominent philanthropists. Over the years, Hong Kong has benefited from the generosity of this billionaire, who comes from a family with a long and outstanding tradition of entrepreneurial success and philanthropy. He has also previously received awards from the governments of France, Belgium, and the Hong Kong Special Administrative Region. As he was a member of the Council of the University of Hong Kong, the biological sciences building at the university was named after him. In presenting the award, Dr. Elaine Ho delivered the following citation:

"Situated at the crossroads between East and West, Hong Kong has a long history of welcoming people from different nations and ethnicities. Many families who came from other places have settled in Hong Kong and, in the course of the past two centuries, worked industriously to help build Hong Kong into the thriving cosmopolis that it is today. Among these families, the name of the Kadoories shines as beacon of distinction..."

The recipient was Michael David Kadoorie. Despite Dr. Ho's address, people of other nations and ethnicities settling in Hong Kong have been few and far between. Since its beginnings as a British colony in 1842, Hong Kong's lingua franca and de-facto official language has been Cantonese, the dialect of China's Guangdong province, where many trace their roots. There was no need for Hong Kong's residents to learn English. Hong Kong's population of more than seven million is and has always been overwhelmingly Chinese.

Michael Kadoorie is the son of tycoon Lord Lawrence Kadoorie, who had been awarded the Most Excellent Order of the British Empire and made Baron Kadoorie of Kowloon and the City of Westminster. The Kadoories have been in the Far East for more than a century. The brothers Ellis and Elly Kadoorie first arrived from Bombay and settled in Shanghai in 1880. They started off as employees of the firm David Sassoon & Sons. Within a few years, they started their own businesses in both Shanghai and Hong Kong. The family made its fortune mainly in the then-entrepot of the British Empire through finance, real estate, and utilities. The business conglomerate is held by the company flagship CLP Holdings Ltd., founded by them in 1890 and in which they still hold a 35-percent stake. The utility provides electricity to most of Hong Kong, and the company also has equity interests in power plants in China, Southeast Asia, Australia, and India. Other businesses that the Kadoories are involved in include The Hongkong and Shanghai Hotels, owners of the world-renowned Peninsula Hotel Group, Metrojet Limited, and Heliservices (Hong Kong) Limited. The Peninsula Hotel Group operates prestigious properties in Hong Kong, New York, Beverly Hills, Chicago, Beijing, Bangkok, Manila, Tokyo, and Shanghai.

In the June 2005 Queen's Birthday Honours List, Michael Kadoorie was awarded a knighthood as a knight bachelor. Among the wealthiest people in Greater China, Sir Michael Kadoorie and family were ranked by Forbes in 2012 as the fifth wealthiest in Hong Kong Special Administrative Region with a fortune estimated at $6.6 billion dollars.

The Kadoories belong to the tiny Baghdadi Jewish community that traces its origins to the arrival of David Sassoon in Bombay in 1833. Often referred to as the "Rothschilds of the East," the Sassoons were one of the wealthiest and most prominent Jewish families in the Middle East. Their immense wealth was built on the trade in indigo, opium, precious stones, and textiles. Reputed to be descended of Spanish Jews, the Sassoons were the leaders of Baghdad's sizeable Jewish community and the treasurers to the Ottoman governors. When the Jews of Baghdad were harshly treated by a new Ottoman pasha, David Sassoon departed with his large family and followers, finding refuge in British India. Setting up the firm David S. Sassoon in Bombay, he deliberately employed fellow Middle Eastern Jews. Families such as the Ezras, Gubbays, Ezekiels, Kadoories, Hardoons, and Eliases were the associates and subsequently rivals of the Sassoons. As the majority of these Arabic-speaking Jews came from what is today Iraq, they were referred to as Baghdadis. By 1864, they numbered almost three thousand in India.

Initially, they acted as middlemen between British textile firms and Gulf merchants. The American Civil War gave Sassoon his big break as it disrupted the supply of cotton from the Southern states of America. The Baghdadis were quick to seize this immense opportunity by exporting Indian cotton to Britain. Expanding to other businesses, they began to rapidly establish branches in Rangoon, Hong Kong, Singapore, Shanghai, and other places in East Asia. By the 1860s, the Baghdadi Jewish community led by the Sassons had overtaken and shattered the dominance of their rivals, the Parsis. Like the Baghdadis, the Parsis were also a small, tight-knit community in India. Steadfastly adhering to the pre-Islamic Zoroastrian faith, they, too, had moved eastward to escape Muslim rule. A notable twentieth-century Parsi was Queen's Freddie Mercury.

The anglophile Baghdadis soon switched from Arabic to English and adopted Western attire. David Sassoon's son, Abdullah, changed his name to Albert when he moved to England. He became a baronet and married a Rothschild. The Sassoon Docks and the David Sassoon Library are named after him. Despite their small numbers, Baghdadis have gained prominence in India and elsewhere. Among them is David Saul Marshall, the eloquent British-trained barrister who became Singapore's first chief minister. In both Hong Kong and Singapore, the Baghdadis and other Jews make up a tiny fraction of 1 percent of the population. Many of their countrymen are unaware of their existence. In Britain, there are the Mumbai-born self-made billionaire Reuben brothers. Simon started by importing carpets and buying real estate while David dabbled in metals trading. Their fortune today is primarily in real estate. Both are active in healthcare and educational causes. In 2008, they funded The Reuben Foundation Children's Cancer Centre at Great Ormond Street Hospital in London and the Reuben Foundation Breast Health Centre in Haifa, Israel.

In Turkey, Ishak Alaton, a former locomotive factory welder, owns one of the country's largest conglomerates. After working in

Sweden for a few years, he returned to Turkey in 1954 and teamed up with Üzeyir Garih, a fellow Jew, to found Alarko. Istanbul-born Alaton started with heating systems and slowly diversified into construction, gyms, and resorts. Beginning with next to nothing, the Alarko Group became a multimillion-dollar conglomerate with businesses including land development, construction, energy, tourism, and food. From a single-room office, Alarko grew to employ six thousand people. The Turkish billionaire has remarked that his Jewishness has had a profound influence on him. In the early 1940s, Turkey imposed the infamous wealth tax ostensibly for the purpose of financing the republic during World War II. Non-Muslim citizens such as Jews, Armenians, and Greeks, who formed the traditional merchant class of the Ottoman Empire, were levied higher taxes and bore the brunt of it. The wealth of the Alaton family was wiped out. The family lost their house, furniture, and business. Only fifteen at that time, Ishak Alaton recalled that the family was left with only some mattresses and towels. His father was sent to a labor camp in eastern Turkey to settle his outstanding debt to the state. To support his family, Ishak Alaton dropped out of school to work. When his father finally returned home, Ishak Alaton mistook the bent, gray-haired man for a beggar. His father had been a strong supporter of Mustafa Kemal and his vision for a modern Turkish republic. When the state he believed in betrayed him, he never recovered. Ishak Alaton, however, is a model of success in a nation that is 99 percent Muslim and a testament that religion is not a barrier in the staunchly secular country.

Jewish communities have been established in what is now Turkey for two millenia. The majority of Jews in recent history, however, are like the Alatons, Sephardic Jews who are descendants of the fifteenth-century refugee influx from Spain. Turkey's Jewish community in the early twenty-first century is estimated at approximately twenty-five thousand, with the vast majority living in Istanbul. As of 2012, Ishak Alaton remains one of the hundred richest Turks, according to *Forbes*.

No study of success is complete without learning from the Jews. The Jews have achieved success in such astonishing numbers way out of proportion to their percentage of the population.

Rank	Countries	Jews	Total Population	Jews as % of Population
1	United States	5,275,000	296,500,000	1.78%
2	France	491,500	60,700,000	0.81%
3	Canada	373,500	32,200,000	1.16%
4	United Kingdom	297,000	60,300,000	0.5%
5	Russia	228,000	143,000,000	0.16%
6	Argentina	184,500	38,600,000	0.48%
7	Germany	118,000	82,500,000	0.14%
8	Australia	103,000	20,400,000	0.50%
9	Brazil	96,500	184,200,000	0.05%
10	Ukraine	80,000	47,100,000	0.17%
11	South Africa	72,000	46,900,000	0.15%
12	Hungary	49,700	10,100,000	0.49%
13	Mexico	39,800	107,000,000	0.5%

14	Belgium	31,200	10,500,000	0.003%

Source: *American Jewish Year Book, 2006* (NY: American Jewish Committee, 2006)

Jewish Americans make up less than 2 percent of the total US population yet represent a significant percentage of the Forbes 400 richest Americans. Below are among the richest Jewish Americans:

Name	Wealth	Source
Lawrence Ellison	$22.5 billion	Oracle Corporation
Michael Bloomberg	$20 billion	Bloomberg L.P.
Michael Dell	$17.3 billion	Dell Inc.
Sergey Brin	$15.9 billion	Google
Larry Page	$15.8 billion	Google
Sheldon Adelson	$15 billion	Las Vegas Sands
Steven Ballmer	$15 billion	Microsoft
Carl Icahn	$12 billion	Icahn Enterprises
George Kaiser	$12 billion	BOK Financial Corporation
Ronald Perelman	$11.5 billion	Revlon
Leonard Blavatnik	$11 billion	TNK-BP
Edward Johnson, III	$11 billion	Fidelity Investments
George Soros	$11 billion	Soros Fund Management
Steven Cohen	$8 billion	SAC Capital
Donald Newhouse	$8 billion	Advance Publications
Samuel Newhouse, Jr.	$8 billion	Advance Publications
James Simons	$7.6 billion	Renaissance Technologies
Eli Broad	$6.7 billion	American International Group
David Geffen	$6.5 billion	Dreamworks Animation
Henry Kravis	$6.5 billion	Kohlberg Kravis Roberts
Stephen Schwarzman	$6.4 billion	Blackstone Group
Ira Rennert	$6 billion	AM General
George Roberts	$6 billion	Kohlberg Kravis Roberts
William Davidson	$5.5 billion	Guardian Industries Corp.
Sumner Redstone	$5.1 billion	Viacom
Micky Arison	$5 billion	Carnival Cruise Lines

Paul Milstein & family	$5 billion	Milstein Properties
Samuel Zell	$5 billion	Covanta Holding
Lester Crown & family	$4.8 billion	General Dynamics
Ralph Lauren	$4.7 billion	Polo Ralph Lauren
Bradley Hughes	$4.5 billion	Public Storage
Stephen Ross	$4.5 billion	The Related Companies L.P.
Joan Tisch	$3.8 billion	Loews Corporation
Leonard Stern	$3.7 billion	J.W. Childs
Leonard Lauder	$3.6 billion	Estée Lauder
Haim Saban	$3.6 billion	Saban Entertainment
Leon Black	$3.5 billion	Apollo Management L.P.
Edgar Bronfman, Sr.	$3.5 billion	Seagram Company Ltd.
Bruce Kovner	$3.5 billion	Caxton Associates, LLC
Theodore Lerner	$3.5 billion	Lerner Enterprises
Donald Schneider	$3.5 billion	Franklin Electric
Ronald Lauder	$3.4 billion	Estée Lauder
Mitchell Rales	$3.4 billion	Danaher Corporation
Stephen Wynn	$3.4 billion	Wynn Resorts
Evgeny Shvidler	$3.3 billion	Gazprom Neft
Steven Spielberg	$3.1 billion	Dreamworks Animation
Edward Lampert	$3 billion	Sears Holding Company
Leslie Wexner	$2.8 billion	Limited Brands
Mortimer Zuckerman	$2.8 billion	Boston Properties
David Rubenstein	$2.7 billion	The Carlyle Group
Mark Cuban	$2.6 billion	HDNet, Dallas Mavericks
Leonore Annenberg	$2.5 billion	The Philadelphia Inquirer
Nicolas Berggruen	$2.5 billion	Berggruen Holdings
Michael Milken	$2.5 billion	Drexel Burnham and Company
Malcolm Glazer & family	$2.3 billion	Zapata Corporation
Thomas Pritzker	$2.3 billion	Global Hyatt Corporation, Marmon Group
Bruce Wasserstein	$2.3 billion	Lazard

Source: List compiled in *Jewish Phenomenon* by Steven Silbiger

Not to be forgotten are the billionaire founders of Facebook, Mark Zuckerberg, Dustin Moskovitz, and Eduardo Saverin, as well as its chief operating officer, Sheryl Sandberg. Outside the United States, there are many successful Jewish billionaires from across the globe. In the United Kingdom, there are Travelex founder Lloyd Dorfman, media tycoon and owner of *OK!* magazine Richard Desmond, fashion retail mogul Sir Philip Green and wife, Christina, who own the high-street outlets BHS, TopShop and Topman, currency trader and owner of football clubs Joe Lewis, record label tycoon Clive Calder, fashion retailer Bernard Lewis of the River Island chain, and Sir Alan Sugar.

In Brazil, the Safra family is among the richest. As of 2012, Joseph Safra has a fortune of $13.8 billion, resulting in his being referred to as the richest banker in the world. The Safras arrived from Lebanon in the 1950s and became owners of one of the country's largest conglomerates, with involvement in banking, telecommunications, and extensive cattle-ranching operations. World-renowned as bankers, the family has interests in financial institutions by way of the Safra Group, including those in the United States, Europe, Latin America, Asia, the Caribbean, and Israel. The origin of the Safra business empire has its roots in the Ottoman Empire. The firm Safra Freres was a financier of the trade among Istanbul, Alexandria, and Aleppo. As a result of the hostility arising from the wars with Israel, the Safras, who are of Sephardic origin, packed up and left the Middle East.

In recent years, a number of books have been written to explain the factors that have contributed to Jewish success. Among them is Steven Silbiger's *Jewish Phenomenon: Seven Keys to the Enduring Wealth of a People*, which notes that the percentage of Jewish households with income greater than fifty thousand dollars is double that of non-Jews and that 45 percent of the top forty of the Forbes 400 richest Americans are Jewish.

Everywhere, Jews have attained prominence in business and are one of the wealthiest communities. Why have Jews as a group achieved so much more than the rest? What is their secret? Evidently, their belief system helps. To Jews, wealth and success are good. The God of the Old Testament is a benevolent God, who generously bestows wealth and success to those whom he favors. Abraham, Isaac, Jacob, David, and Solomon are all blessed with riches. So why not the Jews, who are God's chosen? Had not Jehovah made a covenant with their patriarchs, Abraham, Isaac, and Jacob? In contrast, there are verses in the New Testament that appear to frown upon wealth. Among them are, "It is easier for a camel to pass through the eye of a needle than for someone who is rich to enter the kingdom of God" (Matthew 19:24, Luke 18:25, Mark 10:25), "For the love of money is the root of all evil" (Timothy 6: 8-9), and "You cannot serve God and wealth" (Luke 16:13). These verses from the Bible seem to imply that wealth is incompatible with any devout Christian. Jesus and His disciples are portrayed in the Bible as humble people with very few material possessions.

Obviously, anyone who has an aversion or unfavorable view of becoming wealthy would find it difficult to strive to attain goals contrary to their belief system. Take the Amish of Pennsylvania, who are famous for their peculiar dressing, horse-drawn buggies, and strict interpretations of the Bible. Placing high value on humility as preached by Jesus, they are determined to live simple lives as farmers in their own self-contained communities. Their religious beliefs require them to reject materialism, modern amenities, and personal vanity. You certainly do not see any of the Amish with palatial mansions and million-dollar yachts. Their beliefs make it impossible for them to become rich.

But is success encoded in the Jewish DNA? Let's start by asking the most basic questions: Who is a Jew? And are Jews a distinct race? Today, Jews are found in almost all corners of the world. With the destruction of the Kingdom of Israel by the Assyrians and that of Judah by the Babylonians, Jews were scattered initially in parts of the Middle East. By the second century BC, Jewish communities were established throughout the Roman Empire as well as in its archrival, the Parthian Empire. However, a dispersion of the Jews on a massive scale came about after 70 AD following a failed revolt against Roman rule and the destruction of the Temple in Jerusalem by an army under the future emperor Titus.

Since the very beginning, the religion of Judaism and the Jewish people have been closely intertwined. Over the centuries, converts to Judaism have been absorbed into the Jewish community. There were times where conversion accounted for a substantial growth of the Jewish population. In the first century of the Christian era, for example, it was said that the Jewish population of the Roman Empire more than doubled largely as a result of conversion. The migration and settlement of Jews over two thousand years in various parts of Europe, Asia, and Africa caused Jewish ethnic divisions to develop as they intermarried and accepted converts from the local inhabitants. Tens of thousands of non-Jews are believed to have converted to Judaism during this period.

Wherever the Jews settled, their physical appearance became almost identical to that of the surrounding population. *Jewish Communities in Exotic Places,* a book by Ken Blady, examines no less than seventeen Jewish communities of Asia and Africa that have developed independently of the mainstream Jewish civilization over many centuries. Emigration often induced by persecution have created these scattered pockets of Jews in North Africa, the Horn of Africa, Central and South Asia, the Caucasus, and the Middle East, including the Southern Arabian Peninsula. Not only have they adopted many of the unique practices of the dominant cultures of their host populations, but they have also absorbed substantial non-Jewish genes through intermarriage. The Chinese Jews look Chinese, and the Indian Jews look Indian. Anthropologically, there is no such thing as a Jewish people. Not only don't they look alike, speak the same language, and share the same customs, even their religious practices differ significantly from each other. Modern-day Jews are an ethnically diverse lot who insists that they share a common identity.

Kevin Alan Brook's *The Jews of Khazaria* recounts the well-known story of the large-scale adoption of Judaism by the Turkic-speaking Khazars, a major world power at that time. According to tradition, Bulan, the ruler of the Khazars, embraced Judaism in the year 740, and a significant part of the population followed. In what is now Yemen, Wakia, the ruler of the Himyarite kingdom, embraced Judaism. He and later kings, including Dhu Nawas, successfully propagated Judaism among their subjects. Many of the people of the small kingdom of Adiabene, situated in what is Iraqi Kurdistan, embraced Judaism following the conversion of Queen Helena. In addition, there are accounts of substantial numbers of Turco-Mongolian Avars, Turkic Cumans, Iranian-speaking Alans, as well as North African Berber tribes embracing Judaism. Recorded cases showed that hundreds in France and Germany converted to Judaism in the twelfth and thirteenth centuries. Centuries of intermarriage have resulted in many Ashkenazic Jews resembling Germans and Slavs. Today's diverse communities of Jews are not the Hebrews of the Bible.

Conversely, there were many Jews who embraced other religions and culture. Since the time of the ancient Greeks, a proportion of Jews have assimilated into the wider gentile society around them, willingly or otherwise, ceasing to practice Judaism and losing their Jewish identity. During all time periods, assimilation took place in Europe as Jews intermarried and their descendants do not identify as Jews. With the advent of Islam, large numbers of Jews in North Africa and West Asia became Muslims and were absorbed by the Arabs, Turks, Kurds, Persians, Tats, Berbers, Tajiks, and Pathans.

Like the Jews, Jewish DNA is well dispersed. Whichever genes unique to or common among the ancient Israelites have through intermarriage and assimilation are found today in Jews and non-Jews alike. Genetic testing has shown that many Middle Eastern ethnic groups such as the Palestinians, Lebanese, and Turks are closely related to Jews. It has been hypothesized that many Levantine Arabs are descended at least partially from ancient Jews who have accepted Christianity and later Islamized under Muslim rule. Some Ashkenazic Jews share similar DNA to that of Europeans, confirming that there must have been the acceptance of a number of converts at one point. Many Europeans have some Jewish heritage, whether distant or otherwise. About half of Berlin's Jews converted to Christianity during the time of Moses Mendelsohn. If it is their DNA that contributes to the high rate of success among Jews, why is it that many of these ethnic groups do not share characteristics often associated with the Jews?

The secret of Jewish success is perhaps more likely found in their unique history. Imagine that you are a young boy in eighteenth-century Europe. You reside with thousands of people in a crowded, walled enclosure barely a quarter-mile square. Without sufficient space to build new accommodation, the residents are compelled to enlarge existing homes by building upward, sometimes to the height of four stories. The entrance to the outside world is a gate guarded by armed sentries to keep your family and neighbors in. Nobody is allowed to leave this squalid little enclave except those who go out to conduct business. During the day, your father and some other men leave these walls to ply their trade and sell their wares. Many women and other members of your community have never stepped out of this little detention camp. After sunset, the gate is locked shut. This is also the case on Sundays and Christian holidays, when your community is totally quarantined. Inside the holding pen that you call home is a maze of narrow twisting alleys, disheveled storefronts, and cramped houses, dangerously overcrowded and at times disease-infested; the stench of sewage and urine is everywhere. Outside is a hostile world that loathes you. You and your kind are called "wizards" and "devils" and are accused of slaying Christian maidens and children. From time to time, mobs rise up to lynch or massacre your people. You spend your childhood in the safety of these walls. The shanty slum you live in is called the Judengasse—the Jewish ghetto. Had you lived in the Muslim Middle East or North Africa, you would have fared no better.

You would also have been consigned to the medina, the Jewish Quarter.

An eighteenth-century Italian writer described a ghetto on the malarial left bank of the Tiber River as "a formless heap of hovels and dirty cottages, ill-kept in which a population of nearly four thousand vegetates, when half that number could with difficulty live there. The conglomeration of human beings, wretched for the most part, render this hideous dwelling place nauseous and deadly." This ghetto was the only realm you knew as a young boy. The people living in it and your interaction with them shaped your perspective of the world. If you were ambitious, who would you aspire to be? That would depend on who were the people commanding the highest respect of your parents and the community. Who were the people of authority in the Judengasse? Every community has its leaders and role models.

From as far back as the Middle Ages, rulers delegated their authority. A king could not perform all administrative duties. Not only were dukes, barons, and other nobles empowered by the monarch to govern their own territories, many cities, towns, guilds, and universities became self-governing societies. Europe's Jews were organized on the basis of such autonomy. Despite a despised and discriminated-against minority, the ghettos were effectively self-ruling territories. Within the ghettos, the Jews maintained their own streets, sewers, schools, and hospitals and regulated their own trade and markets. Jewish courts presided over disputes between members of their community, and Jewish judges were appointed to administer Jewish Talmudic laws. And, of course, the ghettos had their own leaders. The Jewish governing body was known as a kehillah and operated in Jewish communities as diverse as Frankfurt, Hamburg, Altona, Furth, Vienna, and Pest. Where Jewish populations were too scarce and scattered to sustain individual communal bodies, such as in rural areas, regional kehillot were established. Who were these influential men in the kehillah? These communal elders who wielded extensive powers were known as the Parnassim. They appointed the judges, rabbis, other kehillah officials, tax assessors, and auditors. They were also in charge of assessing and collecting taxes. In effect, the Parnassim ruled the Jewish communities collectively as oligarchs.

And who were the Parnassim? They were the wealthy elite. The expenses of administering the ghettos were borne by taxes levied on its inhabitants. The election of the richest members of society reflected the influence and contributions of these taxpayers. As Howard Sachar puts it, "With few exceptions, these communal governing boards were dominated by a tight clique of affluent patricians." For any ambitious young Jew, these Parnassim would have been the man you aspire to be. He was your role model. You'd realize that to be that big shot in the ghetto, you'd have to be rich!

In contrast, the fate of the Christian living outside the ghetto was virtually determined by birth. European communities during medieval times were feudal and dominated by lords and hereditary landowners. A person born a peasant would have in all likelihood had died a peasant. Climbing up the social hierarchy to become a lord was virtually impossible. Being a Jew meant that you could, at least in theory, change your station in life and attain a position of prominence in your society by becoming wealthy.

Right until the eighteenth century, the overwhelming majority of Jews were confined to ghettos and had to pay hefty taxes to gain entry into Christian communities. They were also barred from parks, inns, coffeehouses, and immediate vicinities of cathedrals. However, there was a small privileged class of Jews, the Schutzjuden, who in return for a substantial fee had special rights of travel and domicile. But there was an even more miniscule group of "generally privileged" Jews consisting of industrialists and financiers who were accorded by their kings full privileges of residence and occupation, including the right to purchase land and build homes wherever they chose, and these rights were inherited by their children.

In the early eighteenth century, Frederick II, the ruler of Prussia, made it known how much he despised the Jews in his *Political Testament*. Nevertheless, he understood and appreciated the importance of Jewish industrialists and financiers. For the sake of his nation's advancement, he made Jews court purveyors, factory owners, and managers of export houses. Princes of other German states followed the example of Frederick II, who was described as the most brilliant of the enlightened despots. As a reward for establishing new industries and trade connections, these successful Jews and their children were allowed to reside outside the ghettos, were exempted from Jew taxes, and were granted privileged traveling rights. Thus, during this chapter of European history, there emerged the Hofjude or court Jew. Due to their expertise and connections, these Jews were awarded contracts for delivery of silver to government mints and for the sale of cash and bills of exchange and sale. Court Jews also played a prominent role in the various wars as suppliers of uniforms, military equipment, ammunitions, and were even mercenaries.

Samuel Oppenheimer of Heidelberg came into prominence as a military contractor to the Palatine Elector in the 1660s. During the wars between the Habsburg Empire and France, he was appointed by Emperor Leopold I to provision for the whole Austrian army. He supplied Vienna when the Turks besieged it in 1683 as well as during the empire's subsequent campaigns in Hungary and the Balkans. Not only was this ghetto-born Jew well remunerated, he was bestowed the official titles of oberfaktor (supreme supply purveyor) and oberkriegsfaktor (supreme military supply purveyor). His nephew, Joseph Suss Opppenheimer, one of the most flamboyant of the court financiers, made his reputation as a banker for the landgrave of Hesse-Darmstadt. Later, he became the court moneylender, gem collector, and private banker to Prince Karl Alexander of Wurttemberg. Many other Jews in German-speaking Europe became court financiers. In the late seventeenth century, Vienna-based Samson Wertheimer started as one of a number of small moneylenders to the minor court nobility. During the War of Spanish Succession, Wertheimer brought together a group of Jewish bankers including Aaron Beer, Hirsch Kahn, and Behrend Lehmann to lend substantial amounts of money to Emperor Leopold I and his allies. These Jews arranged for what we refer to today as syndicated loans to enable the Habsburg ruler to wage wars simultaneously against France and the Ottoman Empire.

In 1791, Daniel Itzig, a financier from Berlin, was granted a patent of naturalization that extended to him and his son "all rights possessed by the Christian citizens throughout the entire state of Prussia." Similar patents in the eighteenth century were granted to eleven other Jewish households. Behrend Lehman had a palatial home in Cleves, while Suss Oppenheimer furnished his mansions in Frankfurt, Stuttgart and elsewhere with expensive works of art by Rubens, Teniers, Jordaens, and other Flemish painters, precious china, rare engravings, gold vessels, and books. These wealthy Jews virtually became aristocrats and entertained rulers, courtiers, and ambassadors in their homes and at the weddings of their children. These court Jews also functioned as intercessors between their fellow Jews and the rulers. Through their powerful positions, they used their influence to win the en bloc privilege of settlement in Dresden, Leipzig, Kassel, Brunswick, and Breslau. No doubt the ordinary ghetto Jews had to acknowledge the protection and influence of men like the Oppenheimers, Sinzheims, Wertheimers, and Lehmans to improve their lot. As the numbers of privileged Jews increased all over, nineteenth-century Europe, wealthy and influential Jews made their mark in society. Sir Moses Montefiore was made sheriff of London in 1837. Adolph Cremieux became France's minister of justice in 1848. Baron Maurice von Hirsch became one of the richest men in Europe in the late nineteenth century.

The story of the crème de la crème of the Jewish banking families, however, begins with Meyer Amschel Rothschild, who was born in 1744 in the ghetto of Frankfurt-am-Main. His family, who were moneychangers for generations, lived in a tiny, overcrowded shop. While in his adolescence, he became an apprentice in the firm of Wolf Jakob Oppenheim in the German port of Hanover. There, he not only learned the basics of business, but he became aware of the privileges of the court Jews while still in his formative years. The respect accorded to them by both Jews and gentiles alike must surely have made an impression on him. He might not have been totally new to this other world as his grandfather had dealings with the extremely wealthy court Jew Suss-Oppenheimer. The exposure to a young and impressionable ghetto-born Jew like Mayer Amschel was of paramount importance. Carved into the walls of his ghetto was graffito that must have been unspeakably obscene for that conservative era. The scene was that of three Jews, two of whom were rabbis, doing despicable acts on a pig, an unclean animal in the Jewish religion. One Jew suckled the sow's teats. The second lifted the sow's tail to enable the third to drink the animal's excrement. The picture on the wall where the Frankfurt's Jews called home was not just terribly offensive and demeaning, but it was symbolic of the Jews as a despised and downtrodden people. The existence of the court Jews, however, showed that it was possible for an outcaste to be successful, wealthy, and accorded titles and privileges. Not only that, but a Jew could gain the trust and respect of the highest powers in the land. If he only had what it takes, he could be mingling with royalty and high society as if he himself were one of them. It must have dawned on European Jews early that money not only gives you power but respect from everybody.

It was in Hanover that Mayer Amschel began to acquire an expertise that helped him acquire the status of court agent. He became a dealer in rare coins and medals. As it was a trade in which the clients were exclusively wealthy collectors, it provided the platform for Mayer Amschel to become acquainted with many aristocrats and a number of princely clients. Among them was the Crown Prince Wilhelm of Hesse, who became Wilhelm IX, landgrave of Hesse-Kassel in 1785. Mayer Amschel won the patronage of Prince Wilhelm, and he was bestowed the title of "court factor." Gaining his patron's trust, Mayer

Amschel had his first big break when he was appointed to handle payments from Britain for the hire of Prince Wilhelm's Hessian mercenaries during the American War of Independence. While the initial fortune of Mayer Amschel came from coin and antique dealing, his careful savings over the years provided him with the financial resources to move into banking. By the early 1800s, Mayer Amschel had firmly established himself as an international banker to Wilhelm IX and other aristocratic clients. The foundation for the Rothschild dynasty's immense fortune was laid toward the end of the Napoleonic Wars. Mentored in business by their father, four of Mayer Amschel's sons were sent to establish banking offices in different countries, namely England, France, Austria, and Naples. They helped coordinate activities across the continent, and the family developed a network of agents, shippers, and couriers to transport gold and information across the battlelines of Europe. This intelligence service enabled Nathan Rothschild in London to obtain the news of Wellington's decisive victory over Napoleon Bonaparte at the Battle of Waterloo a full day ahead of the government's official messengers.

In 1816, four Rothschild brothers became part of the nobility when they were made barons by Austrian Emperor Francis I, with Nathan being ennobled in 1818. Wars impoverish many, but they also greatly enrich a few. No doubt Mayer Amschel was a savvy man with incredible foresight. But like so many people of humble origins who have achieved unimaginable wealth, the Rothschilds, too, were people with just the right expertise at the right place at the right time. They also had the connections via their Jewish associates across Europe, which was crucial to their success. That network was crucial when he helped financed England's war effort during the Napoleonic Wars. The unparalleled opportunities created by the occurrence of events of such magnitude were obviously not of their making.

Mayer Amschel Rothschild laid the foundation of international finance by installing each of his five sons in European cities to conduct business. He helped invent modern banking by introducing concepts such as diversification, rapid communication, confidentiality, and high volume. Earlier than most, he understood that time and information meant money. Today, the name Rothschild became synonymous with banking and great wealth. From ghetto Jews to titled nobility within a generation, they and other successful Jewish banking dynasties became the role models for future Jewish generations. Marcus Goldman, the founder of Goldman Sachs, who immigrated to the United States in 1848, also came from Rothschild's hometown of Frankfurt-am-Main. Today, banking and investment banking are regarded as prestigious and well-paid professions. However, until the nineteenth century, there was widespread revulsion of Christians and Muslims toward money lending and banking. As Jews were excluded from farming and many other professions in Europe and the Middle East, banking by default became a major Jewish economic activity. Jews not only had a head start in finance, they played a prominent role in developing the science of banking. Jewish recruits in investment banks in the present day are merely continuing centuries-old tradition of apprenticeship and following the footsteps of legendary Jewish financiers who earned their places in history.

Many Jews also gravitate toward the professions, as Steven Silbiger observes in his book *Jewish Phenomenon*. According to Silbiger, 20 percent of the professors at the leading universities are

Jewish, and so are 40 percent of the partners in the leading law firms in New York and Washington. As professionals are among the highest income earners in America, Jewish Americans are a highly affluent group. Why do Jews throughout the world have a history of being drawn to the professions?

On August 2, 1492, the crews of three vessels anchored at the small harbor of Palos de la Frontera were making final preparations for a historic voyage across the Atlantic. The expedition, funded by the Spanish monarchs, had none other than Christopher Columbus as its navigator and commander. The commotion and buzz of activity in the nearby larger port of Seville caught the attention of Columbus. With much anguish, sorrow, and despair, the last professing Jews of the kingdoms of Castile and Aragon were embarking on ships to leave under a decree of expulsion. "A fleet of misery and woe" was what Columbus noted in his log.

Ironically, August 2, 1492, was the ninth day of the Hebrew month of Av. It was a day of fast to commemorate the destruction of the Temple of Jerusalem and the exile of the remaining Jewish people from their homeland. Tragically, this was also the final night Jews who refused to abjure their faith were spending in the land of their birth. The last of these ships departed Spain for good on August 3, carrying with them men, women, and children who must have been terrified of the unknown. On this same day, Columbus's small flotilla commenced its celebrated journey of discovery.

The Catholic priest Andres Bernaldes described this sorry spectacle:

"They went out from the lands of their birth, boys and adults, old men, and children, on foot, or riding on donkeys or other beasts...they went by roads and fields with much labor and ill-fortune, some collapsing, others getting up, some dying, others giving birth, others falling ill, so that there was no Christian who was not sorry for them....the rabbis were encouraging them and making the women and boys sing and beat drums and tambourines, to enliven the people. And so they went out of Castile."

Known as the Alhambra Decree, this law gave the Jews of Spain, who numbered approximately 300,000, four months to leave. They reacted with surprise and disbelief. Don Isaac Abrabanel described the response of his fellow Jews:

"The people heard this evil decree and they mourned. Wherever word of the decree reached, there was great mourning among the Jews. There was great trembling and sorrow the like of which had not been experienced since the days of the exile of the Jews from their land to the land of foreigners..."

Even on the eve of expulsion, there were so many men of Jewish extraction occupying the highest positions in the state. Among them were Finance Minister Luis de Santagel, Treasurer-General of Aragon Gabriel Sanchez, Vice Chancellor of Aragon Alfonso de la Caballeria, and Royal Chamberlain Juan Cabrero. There was also Chief Tax Collector of Spain Abraham Seneor, who was the key person in arranging the betrothal of King Ferdinand and Queen Isabella. Last but not least, there was the wealthy and prominent financier Don Isaac Abrabanel from one of the most distinguished Iberian families. With business interests extending as far as Flanders, he and his father had previously served at the court of the Portuguese king.

The Jews of Spain have a strong attachment to Iberia and its culture. They have been present since antiquity and have had thriving communities since the time of the Roman Empire. Such was the fervent love for Spain that many Jews regarded it as a second Jerusalem. Jews were prominent in all aspects of Spanish life and society. Some of the renowned Spanish-born statesmen were Jews. Their contribution to Spanish culture, commerce, history, science, and astronomy was substantial. Like Jewish Americans of the twentieth century, they were woven into the fabric of society. Envied by the world's Jewry, the Spanish Jews hoped in vain that the decree would be annulled. Abrabanel and Seneor, as the two leading community leaders, worked frantically to have the Alhambra Decree rescinded. The monarchs listened to their pleas. Abrabanel even paid a substantial bribe to King Ferdinand. Ultimately, the decree remained. Jewish chroniclers described the dramatic details of their desperate final attempt:

"On that day, Don Isaac Abravanel was given permission to speak and to defend his people. There he stood, like a lion in wisdom and strength, and in the most eloquent language he addressed the king and queen. Don Abraham Seneor, too, addressed the monarchs, but eventually all agreed not to pursue the matter anymore..."

The Jews who converted to Catholicism were allowed to remain. Abraham Seneor was among 100,000 who chose this option. Since he was advanced in age, the journey into exile would have obviously been too hazardous for him. Upon baptism, he was christened Fernando Nunez Coronel and remained as the chief counselor to the Spanish monarchs. Don Isaac Abrabanel could also have retained his privileges. Instead he forsook much of his wealth by choosing to be steadfast to his faith and joined his people into exile and misery. For centuries thereafter, throughout the world in places as diverse as Turkey, Italy, Holland, Palestine, America, and Poland, even the lowliest of his descendants have held their head in pride and repeated the expression: "It is enough that I am named Abrabanel."

In retrospect, the 1492 expulsion should not have warrant shock and disbelief. Jews have suffered expulsions throughout their history. Spain itself was a refuge for Jewish refugees. Persecution and expulsion were nothing new to the Jews of Spain. As early as 613, Sisebut, the Visigothic king of Spain, issued a decree calling for the banishment of all professing Jews and confiscation of their property. In 1147, the Almohads, fanatical Muslim Berbers from Morocco, killed thousands of Jews in North Africa and made thousands more renounce their faith. When they invaded Spain, massive numbers of Jews sought refuge in the Christian kingdoms of northern Spain. The renowned Moses Maimonides himself was among those refugees. An influential jurist, philosopher, and physician widely respected by Christians, Muslims, and Jews alike, he spent years as a refugee wandering throughout Iberia before moving on to Palestine and later settling in Egypt. In his work the *Mishneh Torah*, Maimonides begins with the introduction: "Since we went into exile, the persecutions have not stopped. I have known affliction since childhood, since the womb."

Following the exodus of between 150,000 and 200,000 Jews from the Iberian peninsula, as many as fifty thousand of those refugees crossed the Straits of Gibraltar. At least a third of them perished, the victims of starvation, disease, exposure, and attacks by local tribes. Many more of these Sephardim refugees would have died if not for the local Jews who provided them with food, clothing, and shelter. Those who survived the terrible ordeal eventually ended up in the slum-like ghettos of the larger cities of the North African coast already inhabited by native-born Jews. While large numbers of expellees obtained refuge in the North African states and the Ottoman Empire, smaller groups settled in Italy, France, and the Netherlands. In the Ottoman Empire, the Sephardim resided in the major cities such as Constantinople, Thessaloniki, and Bursa, where they resumed their prominence in trade and commerce. Speaking Ladino, a mixture of Hebrew and sixteenth-century Spanish, the Sephardim maintained their identity and at times absorbed local Jews. Prior to the Holocaust, Thessaloniki, which today is in modern-day Greece, had a large and flourishing Sephardic community. Among those who settled in the Netherlands, many later made their way to Britain, which was devoid of Jews since their expulsion in 1290, and the Americas. The Sephardim became the first Jews to establish a synagogue in the United States. After the creation of Israel, the situation became dire for the Sephardim who resided in North Africa and the Middle East. Together with their brethren, the Mizrahim, indigenous Jews who speak various Judeo-Arabic dialects, they fled in large numbers with just their suitcases and whatever they could take with them to France, Israel, and North America.

Elsewhere, the Ashkenazim shared a similar story. Ancestors of Ashkenazim originally settled in Italy and the Byzantine Empire. By 1000 AD, they had migrated to northern France and German-speaking states to escape discrimination. It was there that their Judeo-German language, Yiddish, developed. In the fifteenth century, faced with persecution, they moved again to Poland and other Slavic-speaking lands. By the nineteenth century, the Ashkenazim of Eastern Europe grew to comprise the great majority of the world's Jews with the largest community in Russia. After 1825, the situation for the Jews of Russia deteriorated rapidly under Nicholas I. Ultimately, the pogroms and other forms of persecution resulted in a mass emigration to Western Europe and the Americas. As a result, the overwhelming majority of Jews in the New World today, including those in the United States, Canada, Argentina, Australia, and Brazil, are Ashkenazim. Prior to the Holocaust, sizeable communities existed in what are now Germany, Poland, Hungary, Austria, Czech Republic, Slovakia, Ukraine, Belarus, Russia, Romania, and Lithuania.

Moving to twentieth-century South America, by the 1960s Jews throughout the continent were mainly middle or upper-middle class. Like everywhere else, they were prominently represented among the medical, legal, accounting, and engineering professions as well as being business owners. In 1970, when the Marxist Salvador Allende became president of Chile, he set about nationalizing the country's banks and larger industries. Jews bore the brunt of it, and at least six thousand departed for Israel and the Unites States followed by another eight thousand in the next two decades. In the tyrant-plagued nations of the Caribbean and Central America such as the Dominican Republic, Nicaragua, and El Salvador, the Jewish communities departed en

An Honest Look At Success

masse. In Cuba, Castro's revolution compelled the overwhelming majority to join the exodus to the United States. In Argentina, Jews thrived for a while, especially in food products, lumber, steel, printing, and publishing. Others were bankers, developers, and professionals such as engineers, doctors, and lawyers. However, from the Peron Era onward, it was a deeply unsettling period for one of the world's largest Jewish communities. In the violence of 1960s, synagogues were firebombed and homes and businesses defaced. The government's indifference to the violence was alarming. Jews were removed from civil service positions. A morality campaign was launched, and Jewish professors and students were interrogated and beaten.

The late twentieth century also saw the departure of hundreds of thousands of Jews from the former Soviet republics and a smaller number from South Africa due to political uncertainty. Jewish emigration is a centuries-old affair. The ghetto walls are long gone, but the siege mentality persists. There is no place safe except for Israel. Imagine the degree of cumulative trauma on a people who have endured so many expulsions over the centuries since the loss of their original homeland. To be a Jew means that you have no security. You are a vulnerable minority. Any refuge you have was temporary at best. At any time your family could be compelled to move to find new sanctuary. Until Ben-Gurion's declaration of the formation of Israel in 1948, you had no country that you could call your own.

Let's go back to 1492. The Jews of Spain got too comfortable and were lulled into a sense of security. They have been there for generations. They prospered. Spain was home. Now imagine if you were one of the Jews who were about to embark on the long journey

113   E Ong

into the unknown. What happens to your wealth? You try to retain and salvage as much as you can. However, you could only take with you whatever you can carry. You could not bring your house and landed properties with you. You could not bring your furniture and heirlooms that were too large or heavy. If you were a wealthy farmer, you could not bring your fields, crops, and livestock. In the summer of 1492, many Jewish property owners had problems selling their houses, villas, vineyards, orchards, workshops, and grain fields for fair prices over such a short period. The market was flooded with homes and properties for sale in the thousands. The priest Bernaldez describes how most possessions went for a pittance: "A vineyard was sold for the price of a handkerchief, a house for a donkey, a workshop for a piece of linen or a loaf of bread. In their desperation to preserve the wealth, some people even buried their valuables in the hope they would return some day and retrieve them." Ultimately, when you take flight, you could take with you only portable wealth and skills. In fact, since the time of the exodus, when the Israelites had to pack up at a moment's notice and leave Egypt in a hurry, mobility has always been of the essence.

Jews with money and skills were well received almost everywhere. The Italian cities of Naples, Ferara, Venice, and Livorno encouraged them to settle by granting special tax incentives. The Ottoman Empire welcomed them for bringing capital and the latest in European technology. Important merchants, financial advisers, and physicians were given rights of residence. In North Africa, the affluent Sephardim who arrived from the Italian maritime city of Livorno were exempted from living in the ghetto. The rulers were wise enough to appreciate the benefits that came with their vast commercial experience. Chroniclers described the arrival of the immensely rich banker Dona Garcia Mendes in Istanbul with great splendor as if she were royalty. Residing in a luxurious villa in an exclusive neighborhood, she became among the most important Jewish personalities in the realm. Dona Mendes continued to enlarge her business empire, and her agents were operating in all major Ottoman and European ports. With her riches, she funded the construction and the maintenance of schools, hospitals, and synagogues. Rallying the Sephardic merchants as a group, she had the ability to even influence the policies of Suleiman the Magnificent.

The wealthy and skillful Abrabanel, who found refuge in Naples, was promptly appointed by the ruler as his advisor. Abrabanel served both Ferdinand and his son Alfonso II. After the demise of King Alfonso II, he settled in Venice, where again the rulers invited him to the council of state. Abrabanel became a prominent citizen of Venice until his death at the age of seventy-one. His funeral was attended by leading statesmen, and he was deeply mourned by both Jewish and non-Jewish citizens of the maritime republic.

When Maimonides arrived in Egypt, he had little wealth to sustain him. Trained as a physician in his hometown of Cordoba, he practiced medicine as a means of livelihood. He soon made a name for himself as a distinguished medical practitioner. When al-Afdal the vizier of Egypt fell seriously ill, it was Maimonides who attended to him. He became the physician to Egypt's ruler, Sultan Saladin, the Muslim hero of Kurdish origins who was the archenemy of King Richard the Lionheart. By the 1180s, such was his prominence that Maimonides became head of the Jewish community. He wrote many medical tracts that became compulsory reading materials for centuries in European medical schools. Even today, medical students swear the Oath of Maimonides. American and Israeli hospitals and medical centers bear his name. Maimonides was not the only doctor in the diaspora. Almost every Muslim court in the Middle East had its Jewish physician. In 1618, there were more than forty Jewish physicians employed by the Ottoman sultan alone. If you had been a cultivator in Spain, you would have starved or been miserable in the ghettos of North Africa as necessity compelled you to learn a new trade. But had you been a physician, you would have thrived anywhere.

Silbiger said in his book *Jewish Phenomenon*, "My parents raised me as a Jew with expectations of economic achievement, education and social success. I had no shortage of role models from my family, my community, the media and the world. Economic success was the norm in my Jewish community." There is almost no other nation that has suffered as much as God's chosen people. The Jews today are descendants of survivors of centuries of pogroms, massacres, perilous journeys, and disease-infested ghettos. Etched in the psyche of the Jewish people are the trauma and insecurity attributed to their turbulent history. Their collective memory and experience sets them apart. As they are haunted by the echoes of the past, to survive is to succeed.

CHAPTER 6:
THE CHINESE PHENOMENON

One of many books that highlight a glaring fact is Geoff Hiscock's *Asia's New Wealth Club*, a bestseller containing the biographies of Asia's top one hundred richest billionaires in 1997. Aside from Japan, Korea, and India, businesspeople of Chinese descent were conspicuously and disproportionately represented in the list of billionaires in the Asian countries that were covered. It should come as no surprise that many of the richest people in Hong Kong, Singapore, and Taiwan are of Chinese ancestry. Among them is none other than Hong Kong-based Li Ka-Shing, Asia's richest person with businesses employing more than a quarter million people in fifty-three countries, according to the 2012 Forbes World's Billionaires list. However, this cannot be said for Malaysia, Thailand, Indonesia, and the Philippines, where the Chinese are a minority and descended from relatively recent immigrants, many of whom came with little more than the clothes on their backs.

Thomas Sowell's *Migrations and Cultures* also offered some interesting statistics on the world's largest middleman ethnic minority. The American economist and social theorist observed that in the late twentieth century, despite being less than 5 percent of the Indonesian population, Indonesians of Chinese descent controlled an estimated 70 percent of the country's private domestic capital and owned 75 percent of its two hundred largest businesses, including its largest conglomerate. In Thailand, where the community constitutes a larger minority at 10 percent of the population, they control all four of the largest financial institutions that were not state-owned. In both

Indonesia and Thailand, the top billionaires were all of Chinese heritage. In the Philippines, where the Chinese accounted for no more than 1 percent of the population, they came to control an astounding 75 percent of the retail trade and owned 75 percent of the rice mills in the country. With the exception of a few powerful families of European extraction such as the Ayalas, Sorianos, and Roxas, whose wealth originated during the Spanish colonial years, Chinese Filipinos dominate the list of the country's richest. Even in the Western hemisphere, where the Chinese are insignificant in numbers, they have become an economic force to be reckoned with. The Chinese owned most of the grocery stores and other retail businesses in the Jamaican capital of Kingston and Peru's capital city, Lima. Today, Chinese are counted among the richest Americans. They include South-African-born Dr. Patrick Soon-Shiong, who is regarded as the wealthiest American in the healthcare industry, Taiwanese immigrants David Sun and John Tu, who founded Kingston Technology, and Jerry Yang, who co-founded Yahoo!Inc.

Let's look at how it all started. It was the early 1860s, and tens of thousands of Americans were killing each other in the battlefields of the Civil War over the issue of slavery and the right of states to secede from the union. On the other side of the world across the Pacific Ocean, a far deadlier military conflict was simultaneously taking place. By the time it ended, the death toll was reported to be more than ten times that of the American Civil War.

The story begins in 1814, when a boy was born to a peasant family in a farming village in Guangdong province, southern China. The family's surname was Hong, and they were Hakkas, a sub-group of ethnic Chinese. Regarded as the gypsies of China and living among speakers of different dialect groups in small enclaves scattered across six southern provinces, the Hakkas are descended from refugees who fled northern China during a period of civil unrest. Without a homeland of their own, they were economically marginalized and frequently looked down upon by their numerically superior and socially dominant Cantonese- and Hokkien-speaking neighbors. A rugged and hardy folk, they refrained from binding the feet of their women in accordance with Chinese custom to enable them to do hard manual labor. From a very early age, Hong Xiuquan was made to study by his parents, who dreamt of a better life for their son. For almost thirteen centuries, imperial China had a system of selecting a class of scholarly bureaucrats called Mandarins by way of an extremely rigorous nationwide examination. The idea behind this system was that the brightest and most academically gifted young men would be drawn into the powerful and influential Mandarin class irrespective of pedigree, social status, or wealth. As it was based solely on merit, this meant that even the most disadvantaged individuals from the peripheral regions of China had the same opportunity of becoming part of the elite and, thereafter, enjoying the privileges that came with it. The state's bureaucracy would therefore have the best officials to administer the country on behalf of the emperor.

Hong Xiuquan strove religiously to achieve his goal. His childhood and teenage years were dedicated solely to studying. He even became a tutor to children in his village to support himself in the meantime. In 1836, at age twenty-two, he made his first attempt at the examinations. Had Hong Xiuquan gotten through, it is likely that history would have taken a different path. Unfortunately, he never succeeded in passing despite retaking the tests repeatedly. At age thirty-seven, after many failed attempts to gain access to the ranks of the prestigious administrators, Hong Xiuquan suffered a nervous breakdown and experienced a lengthy bout of illness. By chance, he had encountered a Protestant Christian missionary when he went to the large port city of Guangzhou for his last attempt at the examination. Cosmopolitan Guangzhou, or Canton, was one of the five treaty ports opened to foreigners for trade and residence under the Treaty of Nanking with Britain. It was during his recovery that Hong Xiuquan perused with great interest the pamphlet he received from the missionary. What occurred was a life-changing experience for Hong Xiuquan that would ultimately determine the fate of millions of people in southern China. Hong Xiuquan was convinced that he had a divine vision. God had revealed to him that he was the younger brother of Jesus Christ sent on a heavenly mission to overthrow China's Qing Dynasty. Why exactly the God of the Hebrews had a bone to pick with the Qings remains uncertain. The Qings were established by the last wave of foreign invaders from the north. In 1644, a Chinese general had treacherously allowed these Manchu tribesmen entry into China by opening the gates of the Great Wall. Two centuries had passed since the conquest, and the Manchu people had adopted the customs and traditions of the majority Han Chinese people. However, the Chinese, who came from a culture that was contemptuous of barbarians, still despised the Manchus for coming from the lineage of the nomadic Jurchens. This was the mid-nineteenth century, and the Middle Kingdom suffered a series of natural disasters and economic problems. Furthermore, in 1842, Britain dealt a humiliating defeat to China in the First Opium War. The Qings's claim to the universal overlordship of All Under Heaven had been shattered in the eyes of its subjects. The circumstances created just the right conditions for the now charismatic Hong Xiuquan to make his debut.

Like Napoleon, Hitler, and Ataturk, Hong Xiuquan was the right man at the right place at the right time. Large hordes of the poor and disaffected flocked to join the messianic revolutionary. Among them were tens of thousands of the downtrodden Hakkas. Hong's challenge to Manchu rule was so successful initially that he established his "Taiping tien-Quo" or "Heavenly Kingdom of Great Peace" with its capital at Nanking. Controlling large parts of southern China at its height, thirty million people came under the jurisdiction of his government. In the territories under his control, Hong Xiuquan's fanatical followers attempted to eradicate traditional Chinese beliefs, which were a blend of Confucianism, Buddhism, and Taoism, and replace them with his heterodox version of Christianity. This was bizarre considering that the vast majority of the country's inhabitants held strongly to the centuries-old folk religions and had little or no exposure to Christianity. His civil war with the forces loyal to the Qing government, better known as the Taiping Rebellion, lasted from 1850 to 1864. When the forces of this prophet-king were finally crushed with the assistance of French and British forces, more than twenty million and perhaps as many as thirty million people had perished from the fighting and the starvation that resulted from it. The uprising affected sixteen provinces, and more than six hundred cities were annihilated. In its aftermath, hundreds of thousands who survived the unspeakable horrors would leave the devastation for foreign shores.

It was only in 1911 that the Qing Dynasty was finally overthrown in a revolution led by Sun Yat-Sen. By a strange coincidence, Sun was also a Hakka from a farming village in Guangdong. He was also made to pursue his studies seriously at a very young age. Oddly, he, too, met a Protestant Christian missionary in one of the cosmopolitan ports of China and credited his newfound faith as his inspiration for his revolutionary ideals. Unlike Hong Xiuquan, however, Sun Yat-Sen remained an adherent of the conventional form of Christianity and made no claims to being a relative of Jesus Christ. Sun Yat-Sen was also more successfully academically and qualified to become a medical doctor. He was born barely two years after the death of Hong Xiuquan, and it was as if Sun were the reincarnation of the former, given a second chance to finish what he had failed to accomplish. This time around, the British, French, and other Western powers did not come to the aid of the Qings. On the contrary, they defeated them in the Boxer Rebellion of 1900, weakening them in the process. Hailed as the founding father by the People's Republic of China and Taiwan, Sun is depicted in portraits that adorn both countries.

There had been previous waves of emigrants from China. Some of these early traders and settlers went to Taiwan, while others ventured into Southeast Asia, where those who stayed became assimilated with the local population. The indigenous inhabitants did not absorb all of them. Small communities with a hybrid Chinese-Malay culture, made up of descendants of the unions of sixteenth-century Chinese men and their local wives, known as Peranakan and Baba-Nyonya, have survived into modern times in Malaysia, Singapore, and Indonesia. However, it was the poverty and famine caused by the failed insurrection of a Hakka pseudo-Christian evangelist that became the impetus of the largest exodus by far and led to the founding of Chinese communities throughout the world. The vast majority came from the provinces of Fujian and Guangdong. Not only were these the ravaged regions of China, the treaty ports of Guangzhou, Amoy, and Foochow, where these emigrants began their journeys, were situated here. The primary destinations were in Southeast Asia, with smaller numbers of emigrants going further afield to the United States, Peru, Cuba, South Africa, and Australia, especially in the later part of the nineteenth century. Most were young men recruited as "coolies" by headmen called towkay, who acted as emigration brokers and matched them with employers abroad. Under this system of organized labor recruitment, the coolie's voyage to his destination was on credit. Upon arrival at the destination, the employer would initially pay the passage on his behalf. The coolie as an indentured laborer would be required to settle his debt by working for the employer over a certain period of time for little or no remuneration. Many coolies did not even survive the journey. The horrendous conditions of the overcrowded vessels resulted in the deaths and illness of many of the passengers. Some of the later migrants were more fortunate. Coolies who had served their bond and succeeded in establishing themselves in the new land began to send for their relatives and sponsor their passage. There were also migrants who were funded by their village kinsmen to places where they found immediate employment with relatives who had arrived earlier and made it good. Brothers, cousins, sons, and nephews soon followed.

Some of the stories of Chinese migrants are told in Lynn Pan's *Sons of the Yellow Emperor*. In 1884, at the age of nineteen, Lum Yip Kee left Guangdong. His destination was Hawaii, where there were plenty of opportunities for an ambitious and hardworking young immigrant like him. The plantations cultivating sugar, rice, coffee, and pineapples and the farms raising poultry, pigs, and horses were all desperately in need of labor. Upon arrival, he found work as a taro planter for four years. He did not immediately settle in Hawaii but returned to China and thereafter worked for a while in Vietnam with a Chinese business. At twenty-seven, he returned to Hawaii and began to operate two taro plantations, a business that was obviously not alien to him. After some years, he began to venture into the production of poi, the staple food of the Hawaiians. On one of the plantations, he set up a factory for converting taro into poi. Being the businessman that he was, he diversified further into importing and general merchandising, the main outlet of which was located in Honolulu's Chinatown. After many years of hard work, he firmly established the Oahu Poi factory, which would eventually become the largest in Hawaii. One factory after another followed until Lum became known as the Taro King. It must be noted that the Chinese were extremely clannish and ready to help their fellow Chinese, in particular those from their own dialect group. The money for the passage for Lum's trip to Hawaii was raised by his village folk. The employers he apprenticed with and his business partners, suppliers, and employees were fellow Chinese. The assistance and support from his ethnic community was a vital factor to the Chinese migrant's success. Where they settled in substantial numbers, the Chinese would form associations and set up lodges for people coming from the same district or dialect group. Sharing many similarities with the Jewish landsmannschaft, these associations functioned as mutual aid societies as well as cultural centers.

Like the Jews, wherever the Chinese went, the remarks made about them by contemporary European observers were a mix of awe and disdain. James Brooke, who curiously founded a kingdom on the island of Borneo in 1842 with headhunting tribesmen as his subjects, detested the Chinese from the first moment he saw them. The English adventurer's observation of them during a trip to Singapore was: "Their habits are the most filthy, their dress the most unbecoming, their faces the most ugly, and their figures the most ungraceful of any people under the sun... When they move, they swing arms, legs and body, like a paper clown pulled by a string, and to sum up, all their colour is a dirty yellow, nearly the hue of a Hindustani corpse." Nevertheless, the first white rajah of Sarawak appreciated the importance of their contribution and welcomed them in great numbers to his domain. An immigrant from Guangdong even became his steward. With the influx of the Chinese into his realm, Kuching, Brooke's capital city and trading port, began to prosper. Despite his initial apathy, Sir Thomas Stamford Raffles, the Jamaican-born British statesman best known as the founding father of Singapore, admitted that the Chinese were an industrious people. With the influx of the Chinese, Raffles's new colony quickly became a hub of trade and bustling activity. Today, at least 75 percent of the population of the busiest transshipment hub in the world is ethnically Chinese. In Peru, Juan de Arona described them in a poem loosely translated into English to mean: "There is no place where you do not find the Chinese. From the sacking of guano to the cultivation of the valleys. From waiting of the tables to cleaning the streets. He is servant of the commoner, and there is no activity you understand, on which he does not diligently embark. And the people of the country? They are thinking of becoming gentry!"

Time and again, the Chinese were often compared with the other great middleman minority by a successive generation of observers. His majesty Rama VI, the king of Siam, denounced the Chinese as the "Jews of the East." In the seventeenth century, Sir Thomas Herbert observed during his travels to Southeast Asia that large numbers of Chinese traders who arrived in their junks to do business with the English, Dutch, and other Europeans were "too subtle for young merchants, oftimes so wedded to dicing, that, after they have lost, their whole estate and wife and children are staked; yet in little time, Jew-like, by gleaning here and there, are able to redeem their loss, if not at the day, they are sold in the market for most advantage." In the late eighteenth century, the Dutch admiral Johan Splinter Stavorinus observed that the Chinese who ran most of the sugar mills in Southeast Asia shared uncanny similarities with Europe's Jews in the way their business was conducted. While the Jews had their pogroms, the Chinese, too, were the target of riots and other forms of violence from the moment they first arrived until well into the twentieth century. Because of the incredible speed with which Chinese merchants and peddlers made money and grew their businesses, they soon attracted a great deal of animosity and resentment from other ethnic communities. An unintended consequence of Hong Xiuquan's Taiping Rebellion was that by the early 1900s, the ethnic Chinese had become economically dominant in Thailand, Cambodia, Laos, Vietnam, Myanmar, Malaysia, Singapore, Indonesia, Philippines, Brunei, Papua New Guinea, and French Polynesia. What was their secret?

First of all, the Chinese were naturally inclined to go into business, motivated by their fondness for making money. The fact that they had a talent at marrying surplus to scarcity helped. They were always quick to identify opportunities, which they pursued with much enthusiasm and intensity. Isabella Bird, the famous nineteenth-century explorer and writer, wrote: "Whether he was a foot store peddler or a portly millionaire, the whole of 'a Chinaman's life in Java' was devoted to 'the making of bargains'. He was a merchant with 'his whole heart, his whole soul and his whole understanding' we are told. Who 'could as soon leave off breathing as leave off buying and selling" his very thoughts might be 'noted in figures.'"

Secondly, a well-known characteristic of the overseas Chinese is extreme thrift. They were notoriously great savers, and their discipline in denying themselves immediate gratification is legendary. In *The Millionaire Next Door*, Thomas Stanley and William Danko discussed the studies conducted on who the wealthy are in America and how they became rich. The conclusion in this 1990s *New York Times* bestseller was that not all millionaires have a massive income. The average American millionaire got that way by living frugally rather than splurging on fancy cars, expensive homes, and an exorbitant lifestyle. As wealth is what one accumulates, by living well below their means, over time they can amass a tidy fortune. The findings of the research in *The Millionaire Next Door* merely echo what the Chinese knew all along and what was deeply entrenched in their culture. Interestingly, according to the survey conducted and discussed in the book, the ancestry groups with the highest concentration of millionaire households are also known to be the thriftiest and most entrepreneurial and practice a great degree of self-discipline.

Among the tens of thousands of Chinese immigrants hailing from Fujian province was Tan Kah Kee, from Chi Mei, a village inhabited exclusively by the Tan clan. Like many men of his village, his father and two of his uncles had gone abroad in search of their fortunes. In 1890, at the age of seventeen, Tan followed their footsteps by boarding a ship bound for Singapore. By the time of his arrival, his father had already established a small business in rice and pineapples. The young Tan was immediately put to work in the family firm, and it was there that he learned the basics of business. Like many other Chinese immigrants, he worked at a punishing pace. Between 1890 and 1903, he only returned to China twice, namely to marry and for his mother's funeral. It would have been nice if Tan Kah Kee were to have inherited an established and profitable business. But that was not to be. His father had relinquished control of the family business, and, during a period of absence, his father's concubine and her adopted son drove the firm to collapse through mismanagement. Nevertheless, he was fortunate to have received some of the family fortune, allowing him to strike out on his own. Like most of Southeast Asia, the British colonies of Malaya and Singapore were experiencing an economic boom at that time. Tan put his energy into a variety of businesses such as pineapple-canning, rubber-planting, rice-milling, banking, and shipping. Within seven years he had made his millions and eventually became one of the region's wealthiest individuals. Even when he became filthy rich, he continued to live simply and what many would consider as ridiculously frugal. Tan Kah Kee, who died in 1961, spent his last years in a modest two-story building with Spartan furnishings and little personal belongings in his native Fujian province as if he were a pauper. Potato porridge together with vegetables, beans, and a little fish was the staple diet of this multi-millionaire, who could have afforded anything in the world. Conspicuously successful, frugal, and with a deep sense of loyalty to his community, he epitomizes the ideal Chinese immigrant.

Similar saving habits were observed in another community on the other side of the world. In his book *How the Other Half Lives*, published in 1893, Jacob Ris wrote about the extreme frugality of the recent immigrants of Jewish origin with shock and disgust. Arriving in a number of waves from Eastern Europe toward the end of the nineteenth century and the beginning of the twentieth century, the Jewish immigrant on the average had with him nine dollars compared to the average fifteen dollars of other immigrants. Speaking little English, facing discrimination, and competing for employment from Americans and other immigrants, they were compelled to take on low-paying jobs, especially in the garment industry in New York. Their remarkable thrift brought disapproval from most Americans and gave them their miserly reputation. Ris remarked: "Saving has enslaved them in bondage worse than that from which they fled. Over and over again I have met Polish or Russian Jews deliberately starving themselves to the point of physical exhaustion while working night and day at tremendous pressure to save a little money." Ris, of course, failed to see the entire picture. As Silberman puts it in *A Certain People*, "Saving was not an end in itself; it was, rather, a means to another end: to go into business for oneself, or to enable one's children to go into business or to spend the long years of study needed to enter a profession." Unfortunately Ris was not around to see the implications of the propensity to save of these immigrants on their descendants today. The long-term impact on the wealth of the Jewish people because of their saving patterns is immense.

As soon as the coolies had paid off their debts, many of them wasted no time in saving enough money to start off in some type of business. The typical self-made man among the Chinese immigrants began his career as a peddler and ended up as a shop owner. The stories of their success are uncannily similar. As described in Lynn Pan's *Sons of the Yellow Emperor*, the Chinese entrepreneur would have probably started going from place to place selling his wares such as soap, sewing cotton, combs, matches, and other necessities that he could personally carry. Later on, he would expand his offerings by perhaps selling sarong cloth and thin silks. And the next time, he would be seen with a hired help. By working long hours every day of the week and scrimping on his earnings, eventually he could afford to set up his own shop. Over the years, as he accumulated more money by saving, he would slowly expand by opening another shop or venture into other businesses. His children and other relatives who had been apprenticing with him will likely take the family business to the next level. Some family-run businesses would eventually become conglomerates by the second or third generation.

In 1858, an eleven-year-old boy from Guangdong arrived in Singapore with nothing but a small bundle of clothes. Wong Loke Yew came from a poor household in the district of Heshan. Upon arrival, the Cantonese teenager got himself a job at a provision shop with the help of relatives. He shortened his name to Loke Yew and began to use Loke as his surname to signify beginning afresh in a new land. After scrimping and saving for four years, he started his own provision store with ninety-nine dollars. Over the years his business grew. A risk taker, he ventured into the tin mining business in Malaya. Although he lost considerable investments initially, he persevered until he found a rich tin deposit in Perak. That was his big break and the monetary source for his further business ventures. As he accumulated more wealth, he astutely began to reinvest into more tin mines as well as rubber and coconut plantations. When world tin prices soared, he became a primary beneficiary of the upswing in this business. Later on, he ventured into pawn broking, liquor sales, and gambling. Loke eventually became one of the richest men in Malaya, and his assets and investments were located throughout Singapore, Malaya, Hong Kong, and China. He played a leading role in establishing several companies in Malaya and Singapore, including a bank. Loke Wan Tho, his Cambridge-educated son, would also work tremendously hard and, far from squandering the immense wealth he inherited, branch out into hotels, film studios, and a chain of cinemas in Malaya and Singapore.

Like most wealthy Chinese, both Tan Kah Kee and Loke Yew were philanthropists and donated generously to various institutions within their communities. As in the case of the Parnassim of the Jewish ghettos, the wealthiest Chinese individuals invariably became communal leaders and exercised immense influence in all aspects among their kindred. Thus, Loke Yew and Tan Kah Kee were pillars of the Cantonese and Hokkien communities respectively in their day and were accorded such recognition by the British colonial government. Like the Jews of Europe, the Chinese communities were largely self-governing. The communal leaders or headmen were called "kapitan" China in Malaya, "majoor" in the Dutch Indies, and "nai-amphoe-jek" in Thailand. They dictated policies, and their word was law. Wealth guaranteed respect and prominence in both Chinese and Jewish communities even at a time when others lived in a feudal society. In both communities, social mobility was possible through the attainment of wealth.

Another hallmark of these Chinese immigrants was their power of endurance and capacity for hard work. Nobody else had the stamina to work as hard as the Chinese coolie. Chinese shops and businesses in Southeast Asia were opened from early morning until late at night every single day of the year with some closing only for Chinese New Year's Day. A subtle difference that contributed to the success of the Chinese retailer was his willingness to accept a low profit margin from the sale of each good. For him, it was all about achieving volume. He simply put in more time and effort to sell more of his wares. The increase in his profit margins had a direct correlation with his stock turnover. To gain more customers, not only did they sell at more competitive prices but usually gave attractive credit terms. Driven by their hunger for self-advancement, the Chinese had the perseverance and resourcefulness to overcome great adversities in their relentless quest to attain fortune. They were willing to be separated from their families for long periods of time and venture to the most remote places just to make a small sum of money.

Once again, there is some parallelism with the Jewish traders in the Western hemisphere. In the 1800s, substantial numbers of newly arrived German Jews peddled clothes and dry goods throughout the United States, including the semi-lawless frontier regions of the West. From these humble beginnings would come many household names. Lazarus Strauss, a traveling salesman who originally hailed from Bavaria in 1852, scrimped and saved to open a small general store in Talbotton, Georgia. Together with his three sons who subsequently joined him from Germany, they founded two famous department stores: R.H. Macy's in New York and Abraham & Straus in Brooklyn. Other Jewish peddlers were in California during the Gold Rush selling pans, pick axes, blankets, and boots to the thousands who made their way there to dig and pan for gold. Among them was Bavarian-born Levi Strauss, who made a name among the diggers by selling pants. Levi Strauss & Co was founded in San Francisco in 1853, and his product, Levi's, became the first designer jeans. Moroccan Jews who had been traveling on donkeys to isolated Berber villages in the Atlas Mountains for centuries to sell clothing, jewelry, crockery, hides, foodstuffs, and herbal cures were soon found in the hundreds in the heart of the Amazon jungle amid man-eating giant anacondas, jaguars, piranhas, and caimans. Commuting up and down the Amazon River and its tributaries in their canoes, they sold clothes, medicine, tobacco, and other goods to rubber tappers in nineteenth-century Brazil.

Likewise, in the most secluded hamlets and settlements deep in the densest jungles of Malaya, Sumatera, Borneo, and Indochina, the Chinese, undeterred by the leeches, mosquitoes, venomous snakes, tigers, and other wild beasts, could be found selling their wares to both natives and fellow pioneers alike. Not only was the Chinese trader no stranger in the most exotic of places but quite often played a prominent role in the area's development. Soon after his arrival, there would be a Chinese shop set up. The Chinese shop would become the nucleus of a small settlement as other establishments followed. In time, this small settlement would develop into a town. With such work ethics, it did not take long for the Chinese to have a virtual monopoly over the retail business in almost every country where they settled.

Nevertheless, how much success can entrepreneurs attain without the right opportunities present? Chinese immigrants came to the right place at the right time. In the mid-1800s, a series of life-changing inventions occurred in the Western world. In 1839, American inventor Charles Goodyear developed a process to make natural rubber durable. In the 1880s, the German engineer Gottlieb Daimler created the high-speed petrol engine and the first four-wheel automobile. What spurred the growth of the automobile industry and a global demand for rubber was when Scotsman John Dunlop patented the pneumatic rubber tire in 1888. In 1903, Henry Ford together with a group of investors incorporated the Ford Motor Company, and soon automobiles began to be manufactured on a massive scale. Automobiles needed tires. This in turn sparked a rubber boom that Malaya and Singapore benefited greatly from. In 1876, the English explorer Henry Alexander Wickham smuggled seeds from rubber-bearing trees in Brazil and dispatched them to the Royal Botanic Gardens in Kew, London. Some of these seedlings were in turn sent to Malaya. For his contribution to the rubber industry in the British Empire, Wickham was knighted by Queen Victoria.

It did not take long before the rubber plantations in Malaya and other Southeast Asian countries overtook Brazil in production, and Malaya became the top rubber producer in the world. When W.G.A. Ormsby-Gore, the Parliamentary undersecretary of state for the colonies, visited Malaya in 1928, he was so impressed by Tan Kah Kee's tire and rubber-shoe factories that he pronounced Tan's business empire to be "one of the most remarkable in Asia, if not the world." Another resource that was equally significant and high in demand as a result of industrialization was tin ore. Massive deposits of tin were discovered in Southeast Asia, and hordes of Chinese laborers would slog unremittingly in the mines of Malaya, Thailand, and Indonesia. There was money to be made. By the 1900s, Malaya became the largest tin producer in the world, and hundreds of thousands of Chinese immigrants were there at the forefront profiting from it. Many were miners, while others were selling to the miners all their needs and wants. Like the American billionaires Cornelius Vanderbilt, John D. Rockefeller, and Andrew Carnegie, who owed their success to the Industrial Revolution, Tan was a beneficiary of this momentous era of changes in technology. He probably would not have been as rich if the automobile and the pneumatic tire were not invented then. It can be said with certainty that opportunities on such a scale never occurred again in Malaya after his lifetime. Had Tan Kah Kee arrived in Southeast Asia thirty years later, it would have been a different story.

In addition, the British, French, and Dutch colonial powers of Southeast Asia provided the necessary infrastructure, development, and Western capitalist foundation that made Chinese economic success possible. As in the case of the European immigrants to America, hard work, business acumen, thrift, and perseverance could only take the Chinese so far. European capital stimulated the exploitation and exportation of primary products such as rubber, tin, and other natural resources necessary to fuel the industrialization in the West. Vast virgin jungles were developed and came under European law and order. There was a huge surge in the demand for labor. This of course meant that there were more jobs to be filled, more coolies for the Chinese agents to recruit, and more customers for the Chinese retailers and middlemen to sell to.

E Ong

Less fortunate were the thousands of predominantly Cantonese-speaking immigrants from Guangdong, in particular the impoverished Taishan region, who went to San Francisco to work in the "Gold Mountains." By 1851, twenty-five thousand Chinese had reached the Californian shores. This increased to more than forty thousand by 1860. These Chinese miners had to endure a state of lawlessness during the Californian Gold Rush, and many suffered various forms of mistreatment by the white miners, including being robbed of their possessions. Among the unruly masses of gold-seekers were substantial numbers of bigoted whites from the Southern United States. In 1852, the Californian legislature imposed a special tax aimed at the Chinese. This was a major setback for any Chinese miner in California who dreamt of making his millions. Although it applied to all foreign miners, the tax revenue was derived almost exclusively from the Chinese. Unlike white immigrants, the Chinese were ineligible for citizenship. Tax collectors were empowered to confiscate and dispose of the property of any miner who failed to pay the tax. As the average Chinese miner was earning six dollars a month, while the tax imposed was three dollars a month, saving even a modest sum became extremely difficult. Impostors who masqueraded as tax collectors made money by defrauding those who could not understand or converse in English.

In 1854, the status of the Chinese became even more precarious with a decision of the Californian Supreme Court. In the case of *The People of the State of California v George W. Hall*, it was held that the Chinese were prohibited from testifying as witnesses before any Californian courts against white citizens. The decision had the effect of endorsing the violence against Chinese by whites as it meant that such acts became impossible to prosecute. Violence against Chinese and even the Americans who employed them began to intensify, culminating in the 1877 San Francisco Riot. Ultimately, the discriminatory laws and threat of violence forced the Chinese to stay away from competing directly with European Americans altogether. They were soon reduced to two main occupations for which they were stereotyped in America: the small hand laundry and the Chinese restaurant. They were also found in rural black communities where they set up small retail stores in a deliberate attempt to avoid antagonizing the whites. For a short period of time, some found employment as railroad workers when the Transcontinental Railroad was being constructed. Many whites shunned these jobs as it was extremely strenuous work and the death rates were high. In the 1870s, 90 percent of the fourteen thousand railroad workers on the Central Pacific side were Chinese, and they were credited with the dangerous work of building the line through the mountains of Sierra Nevada. Understandably, no business magnate emerged from the Chinese community in nineteenth-century America. It would be almost a century before the Chinese Americans became an affluent ethnic group.

In Southeast Asia, it was a different story. There were a number of bold and adventurous European traders and entrepreneurs who came to this part of the world to seek their fortunes. With special privileges accorded to them by the colonial authorities, they, too, made it good and established prominent trading houses, plantations, and businesses. However, they were present in such small numbers that the Chinese were able to set up businesses in various sectors without having to contend with competition from Europeans. The latter were never involved in the retailing business, which became more or less the preserve of the Chinese. Although the same opportunities were available to them, the indigenous inhabitants whom the Chinese encountered did not possess the same drive to succeed. It might be that the locals did not experience the suffering and hardships that compelled the coolies to leave in droves for distant shores. The more likely reason is that their values were different. They did not hold in such high regard material success as the Chinese, whose ambition was to become rich at any price. The Chinese believed in hard work and frugal living, and these were both patterns that were in sharp contrast with the traditional culture of the locals.

The Chinese of the diaspora were not linguistically homogenous. The nineteenth-century immigrants who originated overwhelmingly from the provinces of southern China spoke mutually unintelligible dialects. The largest groups were the Hokkiens from Fujian, the Cantonese and Teochews from Guandong, and the Hakkas from various southern provinces. The Hainanese, Hing Huas, Guangxi, Foochows, and Shanghainese were also present but in smaller numbers. Their rivalry and animosity against one another in Southeast Asia occasionally led to conflict as in the case of the Larut Wars in the Sultanate of Perak in British Malaya, where much blood was spilled and many lives lost. Ironically, upon the cessation of hostilities, Larut was renamed Taiping. However, despite their differences, it was beyond a doubt that they share the same cultural values.

Since the nineteenth century, in every continent the Chinese set foot on, the Westerners who have encountered them have remarked on their eagerness to make money and the length they would go to find fortune. Such is the typecasting of the Chinese. It has been already mentioned that most Chinese businesses opened seven days a week throughout the year with only one exception: Chinese New Year. One of the most important events during the Chinese New Year's celebration occurs on Chinese New Year's Eve. Families gather together for a reunion dinner considered the equivalent to the Christmas dinner in the Western world. The reunion dinner is a sumptuous feast and includes many traditional delicacies of meat and vegetables. The serving and consumption of these dishes have great significance according to the beliefs of the superstitious Chinese. Almost all the dishes laid on the table for this occasion are homophones for words that have auspicious meanings, especially wealth, prosperity, and good fortune. There is Buddha's delight, a vegetarian dish containing black hair-like algae that sounds like "fat choy" or "prosperity." A dish consisting of fish is often included, the significance of which is in accordance with the Chinese phrase "may there be surpluses every year."

Popular especially among ethnic Chinese in Malaysia and Singapore is a raw fish salad called "yee sang," which is meant to attract good fortune and wealth. Jau gok, the main Chinese New Year dumpling, is believed to resemble gold ingots. Niangao, a Chinese New Year pudding made of glutinous rice, is a homophone for "a more prosperous year." Jiaozi is a dumpling resembling silver ingots and symbolizes prosperity. Leek is usually served in a dish with rondelles of Chinese sausage or waxed meat during Chinese New Year. The pronunciation of "leek" makes it a homophone for calculating money. The waxed meat is chosen because the meat rondelles resemble coins.

Aside from the name of these dishes, many of the ingredients of the dishes themselves have similar-sounding names with "good luck" and "prosperity." Hence, the consumption of these dishes is symbolic in the belief that the family will be blessed with wealth and good fortune as they usher in the New Year.

It is evident that the Chinese's hunger for wealth is insatiable. As if the symbolic delicacies of the reunion dinner are insufficient, Chinese temples are thronged by tens of thousands of devotees on Chinese New Year Eve, who light incense and pray for a prosperous New Year and an increase in fortune. Although they may pray for good fortune to any of the gods in their pantheon of deities, Cai Sen or Choy Sun, the Chinese god of prosperity, is often invoked during Chinese New Year's celebrations just in case all else fails. During the fifteen-day Chinese New Year celebration, red envelopes or red packets called "ang pow" or hoong pao" are given out by married couples to children and unmarried younger relatives. These red packets contain money ranging from a few to several hundred dollars. Chinese children from a very young age will always eagerly look forward to Chinese New Year as a time where they will enthusiastically count money from their collection of ang pow.

Of great significance during Chinese Year are the golden tangerines or mandarin oranges. They are eaten and generously given as gifts to friends, relatives, and visitors. Known as kam, the mandarin orange is a homophone for "gold" and symbolizes fortune. Plants such as kumquat and narcissus, symbolizing prosperity, are bought and displayed around the house. During the Chinese New Year celebrations, enthusiastic greetings among Chinese can be heard with auspicious phrases, in particular about prosperity. "Gong xi fa cai" or "kung hii fatt choi" literally translates to "congratulations and be prosperous." The Chinese typically wear new clothes, mainly featuring the color red, from head to toe to symbolize that they will prosper and have more than sufficient things to use and wear in the New Year.

Imagine if Westerners were to go to church to pray to a money deity and wish each other prosperity and wealth during Christmas celebrations. The answer to the question "what is the secret of the success of the Chinese?" is apparent. The real question should be how could a people with such a mad obsession with wealth and good fortune not prosper? The outcome is merely a logical consequence. We are all too familiar with the modern success coaches and motivational speakers who preach that whatever one visualizes and constantly focuses on will eventually come to pass.

In the twenty-first-century United States, the Chinese have made it good. According to the 2010 US Census, Chinese Americans had among the highest median income among any ethnic group in the United States with a figure of $65,273, which is 30 percent higher than the national average. They also have among the lowest unemployment rates in the country. In 2007, there were over 109,614 Chinese-owned businesses employing more than 780,000 workers and generating more than $128 billion in revenue. Like Jewish Americans, other than dabbling in business, many Chinese Americans have joined the white-collar professions such as engineering, medicine, investment banking, law, and academia; 53.1 percent of Chinese Americans work in white-collar professions compared to 35.9 percent for the general population. Ethnic Chinese make up 2 percent of physicians in the United States and one third of all people working in the Silicon Valley. Clearly education is a major contributing factor to the success of the Chinese Americans, as these high-paying jobs require good academic qualifications. Chinese Americans have among the highest educational achievements and are the best-educated ethnic group in the United States. They constitute 13 percent of the student body at the Ivy League universities and are disproportionately represented among US National Merit Scholars winners. In fields relating to science and engineering, 25 percent of the PhD recipients are Chinese. According to the 2010 US Census Bureau of Labor Statistics, 51.8 percent of all Chinese Americans have attained at least a bachelor's degree, compared to just 28.8 percent nationally, and 26.6 percent of all Chinese Americans in the United States possess a master's, doctorate, or other professional degree, which is roughly two and a half times above the national average. The vast majority of the members of today's community, however, are not descended from the nineteenth-century gold miners but recent immigrants from China, Taiwan, and Hong Kong with smaller numbers from Southeast Asian countries. Many Chinese Americans fall within the ranks of America's middle class and upper-middle class.

The firm conviction that education is a guarantee to success is a centuries-old legacy from the days of imperial China. The Mandarins are long gone, but this unshakable belief has been passed on from generation to generation. In *Sons of the Yellow Emperor*, an example that Cambridge-educated Lynn Pan gave to illustrate the importance of education among Chinese even today was that of a middle-aged Chinese-American woman whose birthday party speech was focused entirely on the academic achievements of her family:

"We have six children... Our eldest daughter, Anlin, got her MA from Wellesley, and her husband is an assistant professor at MIT. Our second daughter, Anchen, received her MA from Smith in sociology, and is working at New York Hospital. Our eldest son, Kun-Ping, received his PhD from Columbia University, and is now chief of the Far Eastern Mineral Section of the Bureau of Mines. Our second son, Kung-chih, received his BS from Brown, and MS from MIT, and is an instructor in mechanical engineering at Brown University. Our third son, Kung-lee, has his MS from Brown, and MBA from Columbia, and is an assistant in the Department of Economics at Brown. Our youngest son, Kung-yeh, is a sophomore in the school of engineering at Brown."

Chinese Americans have become America's new Jews. They fit well into the stereotype and generalized representations of Jewish Americans. Evidently they both share the same success formula. They hold wealth and success in high regard. Thriftiness, self-discipline, industry, and hard work are intrinsic parts of their cultural values. They place a strong emphasis on education. Not only are they intensely proud of their academic achievements and those of their children, they hold strongly to the belief that good education is a guarantee of success. They realize that successful people are professionals and business owners. There are plenty of role models in their communities for an impressionable child or teenager to emulate. They are clannish and are willing to render assistance to members of their own community. Many of these traits are also found in other middleman minority groups throughout the world such as the Lebanese and the Armenians.

Thomas Sowell aptly remarked, "The overseas Chinese have often been called 'the Jews of Asia,' but perhaps the Jews might be called the Chinese of the West. The overseas Chinese are not only far more numerous than the Jews but have played a far larger economic role in the countries of the South East Asia than even the considerable economic role of the Jews in Europe and America."

CHAPTER 7:
PARABLE OF THE SEED

Among the parables that Jesus told in the Bible was that of the sower and the seeds. A farmer went about sowing seeds. Some fell along the path. Birds came and promptly ate them. Some fell on rocky places. Plants sprouted from them, but as the soil was shallow, they were unable to grow roots. When the sun came up, they were scorched and quickly withered. Some seeds fell among thorns. They grew at first, but the thorns choked them. Still other seeds fell on good soil, where they produced a magnificent crop—a hundred, sixty, or thirty times that which was sown.

Much in life has to do with luck. The seeds that produced a bountiful harvest are not necessarily of superior quality or better than the rest. They thrived solely due to their good fortune of falling on fertile soil, without which their growth would be stunted or they, too, would have simply withered away. Likewise, the seeds that fell among the thorns and shallow soil did so not by choice. They merely went where the wind carried them.

On the morning of January 12, 2007, a violinist stood alone performing on a busy subway platform in Washington, DC. For about forty-five minutes, he played six Bach pieces while at least a thousand people walked by. During that time, only handful of people briefly stopped to listen before they, too, hurried along. No crowd gathered. When he finished each piece, no applause was heard. Nobody cared. More than a dozen people dropped some money into his open violin case as they continued with their pace. At the end of his performance, his collections totaled thirty-two dollars. It was nothing spectacular.

But he was no street musician. On that cold January morning, Joshua Bell, one of the world's best musicians, played on his violin worth $3.5 million some of the most intricate pieces ever composed. Just two days before, Bell performed in a Boston theater where the tickets costing an average of one hundred dollars were sold out. The idea of having Bell playing incognito in a metro station was part of a social experiment by the *Washington Post* to see how ordinary people would react. In the words of *Washington Post* reporter Gene Weingarten, "No one knew it but the fiddler standing against a bare wall outside the Metro in an indoor arcade at the top of the escalators was one of the finest classical musicians in the world, playing some of the most elegant music ever written on one of the most valuable violins ever made." Should it come as a surprise that his performance was met with indifference?

Of course it is only fair to acknowledge that it was not the most appropriate time and place for such an experiment. It was rush hour. Most people who walked past were on their way to work and had other priorities. In addition, while the audience at the Boston theater must have been presumably appreciative of classical music, the same cannot be said of all those who were at the busy subway platform. Nevertheless, would it have been different if the crowd had known that it was a renowned musician performing? Does being famous matter? And could the crowd in the Metro been able to differentiate between the performance of a world-class musician from that of a good busker? The outcome of the experiment, however, still poses an important hypothetical question: do we recognize talent in an unexpected context?

How do we even gauge or recognize talent in any context? If an unknown violinist who possesses an equivalent talent to that of Joshua Bell performed in front of the same audience in the Boston theater, would they have given him the same recognition and acclaim? Who is a talent in the corporate world? How do employers identify talent? And are they willing to recognize individuals who do not fit the description of what they are accustomed to?

"We look to hire individuals with leadership potential, integrity, a sharp analytical mind, creativity, and ability to work with people at all levels in an organization." So says the recruitment page of the website of a top consulting firm. McKinsey, Bain & Company, The Boston Consulting Group, and Booz & Company are collectively known as "MBBB" and constitute the top-tier management-consulting firms. Providing their services to Fortune 500 companies and large multinationals around the globe, they fiercely compete against each other in various geographical regions and across a wide spectrum of industries. While it is said that each of the firms has its unique profile and competitive edge, all are famous for recruiting their talents heavily from the highest-ranking universities of the world. Graduates of the top business schools such as Harvard, Stanford, Chicago Booth, Columbia, Kellogg, MIT, Sloan, and Wharton and holders of advanced degrees in science, medicine, engineering, and law from reputable institutions fill the ranks of the MBBB.

It may only be logical to expect that the consulting firms hire primarily from experienced people in the sectors that they advise on. Common sense would tell you that nobody knows the intricate details of the industry and its landscape more intimately than those who have lived and breathed it for years. Yet managers of many years standing in the relevant industry who get into the MBB despite not possessing the required credentials are few. Employers in the consulting, legal, and investment banking industries may be quick to point out that they require the best brains for the job, and academic achievements are a reliable indicator. What about those who are smart enough but didn't have the opportunity to study at an Ivy League school? Is there a Joshua Bell in a subway station somewhere out there not receiving his due recognition? By not giving them the same chance, are employers missing out?

So what? If one is put off with the snobbery of the management consulting industry, why bother applying? So here's the thing. Aside from the highly attractive remuneration package they receive, many consultants eventually join the companies they advise at senior-management level. According to a 2008 article in *USA Today*, consulting firms are highly ranked in the list of organizations that are CEO factories. At the top of this list is McKinsey, aptly referred to by *Fortune* magazine as the "best CEO launch pad." Founded by a professor at the world-famous University of Chicago Booth Business School, the firm has produced more than seventy past and present CEOs of Fortune 500 companies. A consultant from McKinsey has probably a better chance than you of becoming a CEO in the organization that you having been working in for the past twenty years. In other words, you may be better off being in an MBBB and parachuting your way in to the rooftop rather than working your way up by climbing the ladder.

"Graduates at the top business schools typically get their hefty investment back within four years of leaving school," declares the opening statement of a *Forbes* article on the best business schools in the United States. To recuperate your costs within a mere four years could only mean that you would be earning lots of money. While the first MBA program began in Harvard in 1908 with a class of eighty students, a host of universities have since launched their own MBA courses. Any aspiring MBA holder has to consider not only the forgone salaries but also the tuition fees. A MBA from Stanford costs a staggering $275,000. Yet there is no question that a MBA from a top business school is a great investment. A study reported that the graduates of Harvard's class of 2006 on average had an increase in their remuneration from seventy-nine thousand dollars to a whopping $230,000. The top MBA programs have also produced many prominent people. Among the Harvard Business School alumni are billionaires such as Michael Bloomberg and hedge fund titan John Paulson. No doubt the top MBAs are intellectually rigorous and demanding. However, is it always the case of those with the best results getting into the best business schools? What about the many who simply are unable to afford the tuition fees? This is especially so for those coming from developing countries where their currency is weak and financial aid is hard to come by. It is no surprise that MBA graduates who come from such countries are from the upper echelons of their societies.

The consulting firms and investment banks are not the only ones notoriously famous for their selectiveness. The prevalence of "university snobbery" among the crème de la crème of the legal profession is illustrated in a story in the *Guardian UK* entitled "Corporate law firms widen the recruitment net." The article published on March 24, 2011, noted the furor arising from the announcement that a number of top English firms had decided to expand their recruitment to lesser-ranked universities. Freshfields and its rival, Allen & Overy, increased the number of universities from which they hired from to twenty-eight and forty respectively. The problem, so to speak, was that many of these new institutions on the list, such as University of East London, City University, and Greenwich, are nowhere near the top of the university league tables. Traditionally, the prestigious Magic Circle and Silver Circle firms in England, which pay substantially higher than most legal firms, have focused their recruitment on Oxbridge and other top UK universities. The reason for the stringent entry requirements of the top law firms is presumably to ensure that they get the people with the right caliber. So why should which university you graduated from matter if you can demonstrate competence and are capable of doing your job? It's not as if your colleagues and clients care about where you obtained your degree.

But then again perhaps they do. A senior partner of a large law firm candidly explained that one of the primary reasons that his firm remained selective and recruited from the top universities was because of the talents themselves. "They're the biggest snobs of all. If we recruit too widely, they won't come to us." Oxbridge graduates form a large percentage of the lawyers and trainee solicitors in the leading law firms, whereas only a small minority studied at universities outside the top twenty. The announcements of the recruitment by the top firms at these "lesser universities" enraged and disgusted some of their solicitors, who saw the move as another concession to political correctness. In response to the news, one person wrote on legalweek.com., "I did not study at Oxford and the LSE to end up working with people who graduated from Leicester or Queen Mary."

Still others commented that students from these lower-ranked universities were "dirty" and "substandard." Why would there be so much opposition and indignation to the idea of giving to "the others" when one has received the same opportunities?

Dr. Louise Ashley of the Cass Centre for Professional Service Firms has found in her research that top law firms have an aversion to employing candidates who looked or sounded working class as part of their efforts to preserve their premium brand. Image counts. From a commercial perspective, it may be necessary if your clients are top-tier investment banks to recruit heavily from Oxbridge and the Ivy League. Business is easier transacted when you are of the same pedigree. Wouldn't you feel more comfortable with people who dress like you, talk like you, and share a similar background? As those from the working class are underrepresented in the top British universities, a selection process based on university rankings would inevitably have the effect of restricting access to individuals from certain socioeconomic backgrounds. Birds of a feather prefer to flock together. Opposites certainly don't attract.

In an ideal the world, the best man always wins. In reality, it is never a race. Once applicants are able to show that they possess the level of competence required for that position, other factors come into play. For reputation-conscious employers, there is the question of whether the applicant is a suitable ambassador of their company. This is what employers tactfully refer as a "fit." The premier investment banks, law firms, and consulting firms have always been inclined to take in eloquent recruits who are also cultured, sophisticated, and polished. A number of the organizations with the big brand names have a long history of recruiting from institutions of some repute, and when the recruits of yesteryears rise up the ranks to become leaders and policy-makers, their similarity bias ensures that the hiring policy becomes self-perpetuating.

Let's suppose that employers seek the best talent based purely on academic merit. The question is: do the top academic performers always seek admission to the leading universities? Over the years, untold numbers of disappointed applicants have received rejection letters from Oxford University. So when a nineteen-year-old A-level student boldly publicized her rejection letter to Oxford University on January 20, 2012, it became world news. Her letter to the admission tutors announced: "I realize you may be disappointed by this decision, but you were in competition with many fantastic universities and following your interview I am afraid you do not quite meet the standard of the universities I will be considering." Elly Nowell of Winchester, Hampshire, had applied to read law at Magdalen College. One of the thirty-eight colleges and six private halls that together constitute the second oldest surviving university in the world, Magdalen's alumni include British Foreign Secretary William Hague, documentary-maker Louis Theroux, and Oscar Wilde. What caused Nowell to make such a decision?

It is evident from a visit to the oldest university in the English-speaking world that it has a long list of prominent alumni. Statues and plaques are constant reminders to students of the colleges and halls that they are walking in the footsteps of giants. Sir Walter Raleigh, John Wycliffe, John Wesley, Lawrence of Arabia, J.R.R. Tolkien, C.S. Lewis, T.S. Eliot, Adam Smith, John Locke, Albert Einstein, Andrew

Lloyd-Webber, V.S. Naipaul, Vikram Seth, Rupert Murdoch, and countless other famous people all spent time there. Twenty-six British prime ministers studied at this institution that has a history dating back to 1096. Many more premiers and heads of state count among its former students. Prime ministers of South Asian countries who are Oxonians include India's Manmohan Singh and Indira Gandhi, Pakistan's Liaquat Ali Khan, Feroz Khan Noon, Hussein Shaheed Suhrawardy, Zulfiqar Ali Bhutto and Benazir Bhutto, and Sri Lanka's S.W.D. Bandaranaike. Prime ministers of other commonwealth countries include John Gorton, Malcolm Fraser, and Bob Hawke of Australia, Lester Pearson and John Turner of Canada, Norman Manley of Jamaica, and Eric Williams of Trinidad and Tobago. From outside the commonwealth there are Alvaro Uribe (Colombia), Abhisit Vejjajiva (Thailand), Bill Clinton (United States), and the monarchs Harald V of Norway and Abdullah II of Jordan. Forty-seven Nobel Prize winners have studied or taught at the university, including Myanmar's democracy activist Aung San Suu Kyi. Notable scientists affiliated to the university include Stephen Hawking, Richard Dawkins, and Albert Einstein. In 2011, Oxford, a member of the elite group of six universities touted as the "globally recognized super brands," was ranked fourth in world and first in Europe in the Times Higher Education World University Rankings and ranked fifth in the world in the QS World University Rankings. It should come as no surprise that students there feel that they are destined for greatness.

The reason Nowell gave for her change of mind was that Oxford's admission process was against pupils like herself and that the university failed to address the "gap between elitism and discrimination." Nowell was from a state- or government-funded school. As part of the admission process, Nowell attended an interview. It was this experience that she found a put-off and caused her to withdraw her application. In her letter to the Oxford admission tutors, Nowell wrote: "Whilst you may believe your decision to hold interviews in grand formal settings is inspiring, it allows public school applicants to flourish in the environment they are accustomed to and intimidates state school applicants, distorting the true academic potential of both." The "public schools" Nowell referred to are a group of expensive and exclusive schools that constitute approximately 10 percent of the independent schools in England. School fees are exorbitant and beyond reach for the vast majority of the population. They include world-famous names such as Eton, Harrow, Merchant Taylor's, Charterhouse, Rugby, Shrewsbury, St. Paul's, Westminster, and Winchester. Among their former pupils are members of the royalty, corporate figures, and heads of state throughout the world. Nowell added: "It was during my interview that I finally realized subjecting myself to the judgment of an institution I fundamentally disagreed with was bizarre." On Nowell's Facebook page, she wrote that she was hoping to get into UCL.

Located in the Bloomsbury area of central London, University College London, popularly known as UCL, was founded on February 11, 1826. When UCL sought to be incorporated, it encountered fierce opposition in Parliament from the Church of England and Oxbridge. Up until that point, Oxbridge, as the universities of Oxford and Cambridge are collectively known, were the only two universities in England. Oxford's archrival, the University of Cambridge, was founded in 1209 by a group of former Oxford academics after a disagreement. Both universities were in the early 1800s opened only to the sons of landed gentry who belonged to the Church of England. As being wealthy and an adherent of the established Church headed by the monarch were required for admission, Oxbridge was effectively the exclusive preserve of the upper crust of English society. To put it in another way, not only did the graduates of Oxbridge become society's elite by virtue of their affiliation to these universities, they would likely have been scions of society's elite to be admitted. While today Oxbridge is synonymous with academic excellence, for most of their existence their admission was based on social exclusivity rather than intellectual suitability. Thus, the thought of making education accessible to everyone at that point in time made the inauguration of an institution like UCL such a radical endeavor. The founders of UCL were influenced by the ideas of the philosopher and jurist Jeremy Bentham. Bentham, himself an Oxford alumni from an affluent family, advocated that higher education should be made widely available rather than restricted to a fortunate few. He is considered the spiritual founder of UCL, and his embalmed body is today curiously on display in a wooden cabinet at the South Cloisters of the UCL main building. Nevertheless, the UCL project that embodied Bentham's ideas on education received strong support especially from diverse religious, philosophical, and political groups whose members were mostly excluded from England's sociopolitical elite. Among them were Jews, Roman Catholics, Baptists, Utilitarians, and Abolitionists.

Finally, in 1836, the Whig government conferred a royal charter to the newly founded University of London, which covered both UCL and King's College London. The inclusion of King's College, which operated in a similar fashion as Oxbridge, was a compromise with the predominantly Anglican upper class that dominated both houses of

Parliament. UCL became the first institute of higher learning in England to open its doors to all regardless of sex, religion, or political beliefs. It was a breakthrough for that day and age. Reflecting Bentham's vision and the belief that none should be discriminated against, UCL's motto is, "Let all come who by merit deserve the most reward." And soon people of all color and creed came. Among them was the son of a senior government official from Gujarat's prosperous Bania caste. After studying law and jurisprudence, the young barrister would spend twenty-one years in South Africa fighting against racial prejudice and social injustice before returning to the Indian subcontinent to lead the independence movement. One of the founding fathers of the civil rights movement in South Africa, Mohandas Karamchand Gandhi would be proclaimed a national hero with numerous monuments when the black majority came to power. Many other non-Europeans took up the opportunity to study at UCL in the 1800s and early twentieth century. Other UCL alumni who became statesmen in their home countries include Ito Hirobumi, the first prime minister of Japan; Jomo Kenyatta, first prime minister and the "father of the nation" of Kenya; and Wu Tingfang, acting premier of the Republic of China in its early years.

Although Oxford and Cambridge have since long ago opened their doors to people from all walks of life, allegations of admission to the two ancient universities based on social background remain controversial to this day. One of the most highly publicized cases of an "Oxbridge reject" became known in the British media as the Laura Spence Affair. In 1999, Laura Spence, a student from Monkseaton Community High School in North Tyneside, applied to study medicine at Magdalen College, Oxford. Obtaining A* grade in ten GCSEs, she had the top A-level grades in chemistry, biology, English, and geography. As part of her admission process, she attended the interview at Magdalen College. Spence was not offered a place because, according to the admission tutors, there were other candidates with equally good qualifications but who had performed better at the interviews. In one media report, the reason given for her rejection was that she "did not show potential." Magdalen College soon faced allegations that Spence was rejected because of its prejudice against a state school applicant from a working-class region. Gordon Brown, the then-chancellor of the exchequer, who later became British prime minister, accused Oxford of elitism. At a Trades Union Congress reception, Brown, one of the few British prime ministers who never went to either Oxford or Cambridge, commented that Spence's rejection was an "absolute scandal" and that he believed she had been discriminated against by "an old establishment interview system."

Both Oxford and Cambridge have deliberately made efforts to shed their elitist images and have gone to great lengths to show that their admission policies avoid bias against candidates of certain socioeconomic or educational backgrounds. In recent years, they have been quick to point out the high percentages of students from states schools that have been accepted. In response to Nowell's allegations of discrimination, Oxford stated that in 2010, 55.4 percent of places for UK students were from state schools. However, critics argue that most pupils from state schools are from the elite grammar and selective schools rather than those typically attended by working-class kids.

In a speech within one hundred days of his appointment, British Deputy Prime Minister Nick Clegg said: "One of the main reasons I came into politics is it really gets to me that, even though...we are a relatively affluent country, children are pretty well condemned by the circumstances of their birth... Basically, because of where they were born, who their parents were, where they lived they are going to have less chance of living as long as they want to, of getting the education they want, getting the jobs they want." Which social class a person is born into obviously has a significant impact on their lifelong educational achievements. This, in turn, affects their job prospects. For a start, the environment itself has a significant impact. In 2010, Michael Gove, the education secretary, told British members of Parliament that research has shown that toddlers with poor cognitive abilities from wealthy families go on to outperform more intelligent children born into deprived homes by the age of six. Referring to the study by the Institute of Education that tested children aged twenty-two months and again at the age of six years, Gove said: "In effect, rich thick kids do better than poor clever children when they arrive at school and the situation as they go through gets worse." The reason attributed was that poor children simply do not get "the social and emotional support" provided by middle-class parents. Sometimes the line dividing those who succeed in life from those who do not amount to anything is drawn more or less at birth. Like the seeds that fell on shallow soil, clever children from less fortunate backgrounds are indeed unfortunate because, from the very beginning, their circumstances does not allow for their roots to grow deep.

Wealthy and upper-middle-class children are often brought up from young to be competitive and achievement-oriented. They are privileged not only because they are not in financial need but have parents who possess firsthand knowledge of what it takes to be successful. Children from working-class background, on the other hand, grow up in an environment that causes them to develop an aversion toward success and acquisition of knowledge. As British cultural theorist Paul Willis concludes in his 1977 study entitled *Learning to Labor*, they consider educational achievements as outside their class and therefore undesirable. Those who strive to excel in studies face ridicule by their peers. Their surroundings impede their social advancement and result in their being able to only find working-class jobs.

Children see the world through the eyes of their parents. In their formative years, it is those who are closest to them who help them make sense of things. Social class has created a deep divide between "us" and "them." It could well be that Laura Spence was never discriminated against and she was unsuccessful simply because the other candidates were indeed better. For many academically gifted state school students such as Elly Nowell, Oxbridge would epitomize the arrogant upper class that could barely conceal their contempt and disdain for the masses. In Nowell's words, Oxford, one of the world's very best universities, was "an institution I fundamentally disagreed with." As Les Ebdon, the director of the Office of Fair Access, observes, millions of ordinary people believe Oxbridge "are not for the likes of us." Rather than losing their personal dignity by betraying their roots and social class, they choose to forgo an almost assured bright future as Oxbridge graduates, to their own disadvantage. Still others because of low self-esteem are simply overawed by the very thought of being in alien surroundings that they have concluded are hostile toward them and their kind. In his article "How to break the stranglehold public schools have on Oxbridge entrance" in the *Guardian*, Peter Wilby explains the reason for the dominance of independent school pupils:

"Those students already know many of their fellow undergraduates and can share in-jokes, catchphrases, memories and social contacts. They feel instantly at home in Oxbridge colleges which look like their schools. Their teaching was specifically geared to Oxbridge requirements. It is hardly surprising that 18-year-olds from northern comprehensives fear being out of place... The peer group — and a sense of who belongs on which territory — is of paramount importance to an 18-year-old. It explains why, in the inner-city, so many join gangs. Elite universities provide territory for gangs formed in public schools." To put it simply, working-class children do not find themselves fitting in at the top universities.

In addition, those who are wealthy are accustomed to having and expecting the best things in life that money can buy. Affluent parents are able to afford to send their children to better schools, which gives them a significant advantage. The quality of teaching obviously makes a huge impact on the performance of any pupil. Not only is the quality of teaching in the private schools often much higher than that of state schools, but, more importantly, the students are in an environment where there is a strong expectation from their teachers and peers to enter a reputable university. Gaining places at Oxbridge remains a primary focus for many private and selective state schools. They would often hear about their seniors getting accepted into this or that university. The rich kids have a head start because they have savvy parents and teachers who have a track record of successfully assisting many past pupils to gain admission at top universities. They are given clear goals in life and encouraged to dream big. Since these students were young, their insightful mentors have already sowed the seeds.

Students from public schools who do not make the cut for Oxbridge often gain admission to other prestigious universities such as Bristol, Exeter, York, Durham, St. Andrews, Warwick, London School of Economics and Political Science (LSE), Imperial College, King's College, and UCL. Founded in 1895 by members of the Fabian Society, a British socialist organization, the LSE is famous for its left-wing roots. Sidney Webb, its principal founder, was a member of the Labour Party and lifelong supporter of the Soviet Union who studied for his law degree while holding on to a day job. With their rise to the top of the university league tables, both LSE and UCL have become popular destinations for public school pupils.

The figures in tables A and B below are compiled by the Higher Education Statistics Agency for 2008/2009.

TABLE A		
University	% from state schools	% from low participation neighborhoods
Bristol	60.0	3.4
Cambridge	59.3	3.7
Durham	59.2	4.6
Edinburgh	70.8	N/A
Exeter	70.9	4.0
Imperial College	62.1	4.4
King's College	71.7	3.7
LSE	70.1	4.5
Nottingham	69.6	5.6
Oxford	54.7	2.7
UCL	64.1	3.4
St Andrews	60.7	N/A

| Warwick | 76.6 | 5.5 |
| York | 79.4 | 7.2 |

The list in Table A comprises of some of the highest-ranked UK institutions in the universities league tables. These members of the prestigious Russell Group have among the highest percentage of their undergraduates coming from private schools.

TABLE B		
University	% from state schools	% from low participation neighborhoods
Anglia Ruskin	97.3	17.0
Bedfordshire	99.0	12.1
Birmingham City	97.2	14.9
Bolton	99.8	24.3
Canterbury Christ Church	96.4	15.9
Central Lancashire	97.7	15.5
Chester	97.5	13.5
Cumbria	97.8	15.5
De Monfort	97.7	11.5
Derby	96.8	20.6
Edge Hill	99.0	21.3
East London	98.4	10.0
Greenwich	97.9	10.8
Huddersfield	98.2	16.7
Liverpool Hope	98.3	18.6
Liverpool John Moores	95.2	17.2
London Metropolitan	96.6	7.6
London South Bank	98.7	9.7
Manchester Metropolitan	96.2	15.7
Salford	98.2	21.0
Sheffield Hallam	96.7	17.7
Staffordshire	98.0	21.3
Sunderland	98.1	25.7
Teeside	99.1	26.7

E Ong

Thames Valley	98.7	7.7
Winchester	95.3	11.9
Wolverhampton	99.5	21.6
Worcester	97.3	9.5

The list in Table B comprises of some of the lowest-ranked UK institutions in the universities league tables. Coincidentally, they also have among the highest percentages of state school pupils as well as those from low-participation neighborhoods among their undergraduate students.

A study by Sutton Trust published in 2007 disclosed some startling statistics. Each year, approximately 33 percent of all British students commencing their undergraduate degrees at Oxford or Cambridge come from just one hundred schools, of which 80 percent are private. Further, nearly one in every six Oxbridge entrants studied at only one of thirty schools. Eton and Westminster, two of Britain's leading independent schools, each sends approximately one hundred pupils to Oxbridge each year. Overall, 48 percent of all Oxbridge entrants come from two hundred schools, while thirty-five hundred other schools accounted for the remaining 52 percent. It is no exaggeration to say that a small number of schools contribute such a phenomenally large number of British university entrants to Oxbridge. The Sutton Trust report, which was complied by researching which universities one million British students went to over five years, concluded that "a small cadre of elite 'feeder' schools dominates Oxbridge admissions." The proportion of private school pupils who gain entry to Oxbridge is also truly remarkable. According to the report, private schools made up merely 7 percent of all schools, and their pupils accounted for 15 percent of A-level candidates. Yet, in 2006, only 54 percent of the approximately three thousand British undergraduates who were admitted to Oxford were from state schools. It was the same story in Cambridge, where 56 percent of about three thousand places went to state school pupils. Even so, the research shows that these state schools were either academically selective or situated in the middle-class areas. The statistics clearly show that your probability of getting into Oxbridge is much higher if you had enrolled your child at one of these elite private schools. If gaining admission to Oxbridge is an accurate measure of one's intelligence, what does that tell us? Rich kids are far smarter than poor kids?

Sir Peter Lampl, chairman of the Sutton Trust, said, "It is deeply worrying—not to mention a sad waste of talent—that the chances of reaching one of these highly selective universities are much greater for those who attend a small number of the country's elite schools, mainly fee–paying." The study by Sutton Trust disclosed that the same admission pattern was seen at other British universities at the top of the league tables. These other universities included in the so-called "Sutton Trust 13" were Birmingham, Bristol, Durham, Edinburgh, Imperial College, UCL, LSE, Nottingham, St. Andrews, Warwick, and York. The lack of access to good schools among the children of working-class parents is an important factor that perpetuates the class divide across generations. The Sutton Trust, an educational charity, was set up in the United Kingdom in 1997 by Lampl, a millionaire philanthropist and Oxford alumni, to improve social mobility by addressing educational disadvantage. The proportion of students going to Oxbridge from the top thirty private schools is almost double that of the best thirty state schools despite similar average A-level scores, according to the Sutton Trust report. Research also found that many state pupils with good exam grades did not even contemplate applying to the top universities.

Realizing that children from working-class families lack the necessary guidance, the Sutton Trust's pioneering program was a summer school where hundreds of bright students from non-privileged backgrounds got to experience what life is like at a reputable university. Bristol, Cambridge, Nottingham, and St. Andrews participated in the program, and they were later joined by Durham, Imperial College, and UCL. A 2012 report published by the Sutton Trust concluded that summer school attendees were more likely to get into a top university compared to children with similar academic and social backgrounds who did not attend. Researchers at the University of Bristol further revealed that in fact 76 percent of children who attended summer school were eventually admitted to a leading university. Education transforms lives. But before that happens, there has to be a change in perception and mindset. Many children from disadvantaged backgrounds are clueless about goals in life and have no direction. There are proportionately fewer of them in top universities in part because fewer of them aspire to get in. For the working-class kids who attended the Sutton Trust summer school program, it was truly an intervention. They were like young plants uprooted from a rocky place and replanted into fertile soil.

Ultimately, it is all in the trajectory. Children from wealthy homes have astute parents who aim high on their behalf. It begins with their enrollment in top schools, where they are made aware of and appreciate prestigious brand names from a tender age. This leads them to apply for admission to top universities. Top companies recruit their graduates from top universities. Over time, they are able to compile top-notch resumes that top employers seek. Eventually, many make it to top positions in companies at the top of their industries that pay them top dollars. It is a chain of causation whereby each event is the result of the preceding event. Doing business is made easier as they have access to former classmates, fellow alumni, and ex-colleagues who also hold top positions in client companies and with business partners. Sharing a common background that they are intensely proud of, such as a prestigious school, university, or company, makes them go to extraordinary lengths to support one another. Their commonality with other successful people is an important contributing factor to their success. Business is about relationships. Even mere connections are inadequate. In an intensely competitive world, we need all the help we can get. This knowledge is fundamental to rich kids whose parents impart to them their own formula for success. Many poor kids are unable to grasp its importance. Who you meet at university may also change your life. Look no further than Prince William and the former Kate Middleton.

Rich parents are not only buying a good education for their children. Other than access to unrivaled opportunities, the experience of being in Oxbridge or some other world-class university for that matter is in itself empowering. Years of continuous affirmation by being in an iconic institution does wonders to your self-esteem. It gives you the confidence that you can do anything and everything that you set out to do. The world is your oyster, and nothing is beyond your reach. You have been told that you are meant for great things. You believe them, and your accomplishments become a self-fulfilling prophecy. Your success is almost certain because you were nurtured on fertile soil. A long list of celebrities studied at Oxbridge and found success in careers that have little or no relation to their fields of study. They include Hugh Grant, Kate Beckinsdale, Dudley Moore, Michael Palin, and Imran Khan. Rowan Atkinson, better known as Mr. Bean, studied engineering at Oxford. Sacha Baron Cohen, widely known for playing the characters Ali G, Borat, and Bruno, read history in Cambridge.

Across the Atlantic, it is no mere coincidence that the town in Massachusetts in which Harvard is situated is also named Cambridge. Many of its founders and its first benefactor were Cambridge alumni. Founded in 1636, Harvard has produced through the centuries a long line of US presidents and political leaders, including John Hancock, John Adams, John Quincy Adams, Rutherford B. Hayes, Theodore Roosevelt, John F. Kennedy, Al Gore, George W. Bush, and Barack Obama. Outside the United States, notable Harvard alumni include many heads of states. Admiral Isoroku Yamamoto, the commander of the Japanese First Air Fleet that launched the 353 planes against Pearl Harbor on December 7, 1941, was a Harvard alumnus. So were President Franklin D. Roosevelt, who condemned the attack as "a date which will live in infamy," and General Tadamichi Kuribayashi, the commander of the Japanese troops during the bloody Battle of Iwo Jima who achieved posthumous fame through the 2006 movie *Letter from Iwo Jima*. So what is the big deal? Is it not amazing that so many people from the top universities play such pivotal roles in major world events? Did they get into Harvard because they are extraordinary? Or was it the Harvard factor that propelled them to do extraordinary things?

"Whoever has will be given more and they will have an abundance. Whoever does not have, even what they have will be taken from them" (Matthew 13:12). More than two thousand years have passed since the parable was told, but the message still resonates and holds true.

EPILOGUE

At the center of Kitakyushu in Fukuoka Prefecture is the little-known municipality of Kokura. On the morning of August 9, 1945, this ancient castle town was the target of *Bock's Car*, a B-29 Superfortress carrying the world's first plutonium bomb, nicknamed Fat Man. Just three days earlier, a uranium bomb had been dropped on Hiroshima by another Superfortress, the *Enola Gay*. The mission to bomb Kokura was similar to that of Hiroshima, and the crew of *Bock's Car*, led by Major Charles Sweeney, was instructed to drop the bomb only if they had a clear visual of the target. Two B-29s flew ahead as weather scouts reported that the target was clear. However, one of the planes in the mission piloted by the group's operations officer failed to make the rendezvous at Yakushima. *Bock's Car* and its accompanying instrumentation plane waited and circled for forty minutes. Conscious that they were behind schedule, *Bock's Car* finally proceeded to Kokura. By the time they arrived at about 10:30 a.m., a cloud had partially obscured the city. Apparently this was attributed to smoke coming from a nearby town that was attacked in an air raid the previous day. Sweeney's crew had difficulty identifying the target clearly, and after three attempts with the bomb bays open, *Bock's Car*, with fuel running low, gave up on Kokura and headed for its secondary target, Nagasaki. The rest is history. The phrase "Kokura's luck" was coined as a reminder of how one city's luck is another's misfortune.

The series of events that led to one of the world's most horrific events began with one man. Kanji Ishiwara was a lieutenant colonel in the Imperial Japanese Army, stationed in the Chinese province of

Manchuria. A devout Nichiren Buddhist, Ishiwara believed that a golden era of human culture would be ushered in by a period of massive conflict. On September 18, 1931, a small explosion occurred on the tracks of the Japanese-controlled Southern Manchuria Railway in Mukden. Alleging that Chinese soldiers were responsible, Ishiwara, the man behind the sabotage, ordered Japanese troops to attack the Chinese military barracks in nearby Liutaokou. Without informing his superior or the Imperial Japanese Army general staff in Tokyo, he and his fellow conspirators instructed Japanese units to seize control of Manchuria. Although the unauthorized invasion caused great concern to Japan's political leaders, the magnitude of its success won the support of right-wing and ultranationalist Japanese military officers. Rather than being executed for insubordination, Ishiwara was promoted to head a regiment. The successful occupation of Manchuria soon led to a full-scale invasion of China with more than three million Japanese soldiers deployed. That was how World War II began in Asia.

The Japanese invasion was for Mao Zedong what the French Revolution was for Napoleon. As Daniel Moran pointed out in his *Wars of National Liberation*, in 1934 the heavily outnumbered Red Army was on the brink of destruction and began a retreat through thousands of miles in western China to escape their enemies. Known as the Long March, it became a defining moment in the history of the People's Republic of China. Although it is now made to be a heroic epic, only one-tenth who left Jiangxi under Mao made it to the destination. Not only did the 1936 Japanese invasion save the Communists from annihilation, but when World War II ended, the tables were turned, with the Communists having the upper hand. The Nationalists, which did most of the fighting, lost many of their best troops and a large number of highly trained officers. While the Nationalists, who fought the Japanese using conventional warfare, met with little success, the guerilla tactics employed by the Communists were very effective, resulting in large areas of the countryside coming under their control. The material and financial resources of the Nationalists were also decimated by the war. However, the subsistence economy of the Communist-controlled countryside remained relatively intact. Toward the end of the war, the Soviets, who captured Manchuria, took possession of vast quantities of Japanese equipment sufficient to arm 600,000 Communist troops. Mao could have easily shared a similar fate as Paoli and other forgotten revolutionaries if not for this stroke of luck. Ishiwara survived the war and was never charged with war crimes. The unintended consequences of his actions were that the world's most populous nation came under Communist rule.

Bibliography and Further Reading

Introduction: One Man's Vision

Dr. Tim Dowley (organizing editor) with John H.Y. Briggs, Dr. Robert Linder, and David F. Wright (consulting editors), *A Lion Handbook of Christianity* (Lion Publishing, 1990)

William Dalrymple, *From the Holy Mountain, A journey among the Christians of the Middle East* (Henry Holt and Company, 1999)

Timothy D. Barnes, *Constantine and Eusebius* (Harvard University Press, 1981)

Timothy D. Barnes, *The New Empire of Diocletian and Constantine* (Harvard University Press, 1982)

Averil Cameron and Stuart G. Hall, *Life of Constantine* (Oxford: Clarendon Press, 1989)

Noel Lenski, *The Cambridge Companion to the Age of Constantine* (New York: Cambridge University Press, 2006)

Oliver Nicholson, "Constantine's Vision of the Cross" (*Vigiliae Christianae*, 54:3, 2000)

Charles Matson Odahl, *Constantine and the Christian Empire* (New York: Routledge, 2004)

John Holland Smith, *Constantine the Great* (London: Hamish Hamilton, 1971)

Chapter 1: Head Start

Terry Laughlin with John Delves, *Total Immersion, The revolutionary way to swim better, faster and easier* (Fireside, Simon & Schuster, 1996)

Andrew Prince, "The science behind swimmers' dolphin kick" (*NPR* August 13, 2008)

Bruce Arthur, "Phelps wins seventh gold by the absolute smallest of margins" (*National Post*, August 15, 2008)

Caroll Trosclair, "Michael Phelps Sponsorships Olympic Swim Champ already making millions as corporate spokesman" (suite101.com, August 19, 2008)

"How Michael Phelps managed to break so many swimming records, one after another" (MunFitnessBlog.com, August 20, 2008)

Michael Phelps, Beneath the Surface (United States: Sports Publishing LLC, 2004)

Michael Phelps, No Limits: The Will to Succeed (United States: Free Press, 2008)

Bob Schaller, Michael Phelps: The Untold Story of a Champion (United States: St. Martin's Griffin, 2008)

"Phelps picks up third gold medal in Beijing" (*The Belfast Telegraph*, August 12, 2008)

"More gold and another day at the office for Michael Phelps" (*Daily News*, New York, August 12, 2008)

Jason Stallman, "Phelps Adds 2 More Gold Medals" (*The New York Times*, August 12, 2008)

Jason Stallman, "Phelps wins 200 individual medley for sixth gold" (*The New York Times*, August 15, 2008)

"Michael Phelps overtakes Mark Spitz with record-breaking haul of eight gold medals" (*The Sunday Telegraph*, London, August 17, 2008)

Rebecca Bryan, "Phelps savours triumph over rival Cavic" (*The Sydney Morning Herald*, August 2, 2009)

John Kenny , "Phelps goes under 50 seconds in 100 m butterfly" (*The Irish Times*, August 3, 2009)

Scott M. Reid, "Controversial O.C. Serb could spoil Phelps' gold rush" (*The Orange County Register*, August 14, 2008)

Enith Brigitha (www.sports-reference.com)

Mike Gustafson, "Acknowledging Enith Brigitha," usaswimming.org, (February 15, 2012),

CullenJones.com—Official website of Cullen Jones

Parting the Waters, Documentary film about Cullen Jones at DoTell Productions.com

Howard Sounes, The Wicked Game: Arnold Palmer, Jack Nicklaus, Tiger Woods and the Story of Modern Golf (Harper Collins, 2004)

Tom Callahan, *His Father's Son: Earl and Tiger Woods* (2010)

"Earl Woods" (*The Telegraph*, June 5, 2006)

Earl Woods and Pete McDaniel, *Training a Tiger: Raising a Winner in Golf and in Life* (1997)

Tiger Woods, *How I Play Golf* (Warner Books, New York, 2001)

E Ong

"Zimbabwe puts aside racial tensions to give hero's welcome to triple medal winner" (*USA Today*, August 25, 2004)

Kirsty Coventry: Success brings rare cheer to Zimbabwe (Australian Broadcasting Corporation, 6 June 2008)

BBC News, "Africa/Zimbabwe swimmer gets cash prize" (August 29, 2008)

Chapter 2: Perfect Timing

Martin Windrow and Francis K. Mason, *The World's Greatest Military Leaders* (Grange Books, 2000)

William Doyle, *The French Revolution: A very short introduction* (Oxford University Press, 2001)

William Doyle, *The Oxford history of the French Revolution* (Oxford University Press, 2002)

Linda Frey and Marsha Frey, *The French Revolution* (Greewood Press, Connecticut, 2004)

Francois Furet, Revolutionary France, 1770-1880 (Blackwell Publishing, 1995)

Christopher Hibber, *The Days of the French Revolution* (New Tork: Quill, William Morrow, 1980)

Lynn Hunt, Politics, Culture and Class in the French Revolution (University of California Press, Berkeley, 1984)

Emmet Kennedy, *A Cultural History of the French Revolution* (Yale University Press, New Haven, 1989)

Sylvia Neely, *A Concise History of the French Revolution* (Rowman & Littlefield, 2008)

George Rude, *The French Revolution: Its Causes, Its History and Its Legacy After 200 Years* (Grove Press, 1991)

Albert Soboul, *A short history of the French Revolution: 1789-1799* (University of California Press, Ltd, 1977)

Richard Mackey, "American Revolutionary influences on the French Revolution," (*Conspectus of History* 1(3): 57, 1976)

Steven Kaplan, *The Famine Plot Persuasion in Eighteenth-Century France* (Diane Publishing Co, Pennsylvania, 1982)

Richard Grove, "Global Impact of the 1789-93 El Nino" (*Nature* 393: 318-319, 1998)

John Abbott, *Life of Napoleon Bonaparte* (Kessinger Publishing, 2005)

E Ong

Christon I. Archer, John R. Ferris, Holder H. Herwig, World History of Warfare (University of Nebraska Press, 2002)

Rafe Blaufarb, *Napoleon: Symbol for an Age, A Brief History with Documents* (Bedford, 2007)

David Chandler, *The Campaigns of Napoleon* (Simon & Schuster, 1995)

David Chandler, *Napoleon* (Leo Cooper, 2002)

Owen Connelly, *Blundering to Glory: Napoleon's Military Campaigns* (Rowman & Littlefield, 2006)

Philip Dwyer, *Napoleon: The Path to Power 1769-1799* (Bloomsbury, 2008)

Vincent Cronin, *Napoleon* (HarperCollins, 1994)

Felix Markham, *Napoleon* (Mass Market Paperback, 1988)

Frank McLynn, *Napoleon* (Pimlico, 1988)

Feroz Ahmad, *The Making of Modern Turkey* (Routledge, London & New York, 1993)

Patrick Kinross, *Ataturk: The Rebirth of a Nation* (London: Phoenix Press, 2003)

Andrew Mango, *Ataturk: The Biography of the Founder of Modern Turkey* (Overlook Press, Peter Mayer Publishers Inc., Woodstock, New York, 2002)

Andrew Mango, *Ataturk* (London: John Murray, 2004)

Chapter 3: Even Geniuses Need a Little Help

Lindsey Fraser, "Harry and me" (*The Scotsman*, November 2, 2002)

Bernard Bruce, *Vincent by Himself* (Time Warner, London, 2004)

Philip Callow, *Vincent van Gogh: A Life* (Chicago: Ivan R. Dee, 1990)

Kathleen Powers Erickson, *At Eternity's Gate: The Spiritual Vision of Vincent van Gogh* (1998)

Martin Gayford, *The Yellow House: Van Gogh, Gauguin and Nine Turbulent Weeks in Arles* (Penguin, London, 2006)

David I. *Grossvogel, Behind the Van Gogh Forgeries: A Memoir by David I. Grossvogel* (Author's Choice Press, San Jose, 2001)

A.M. Hammacher, *Vincent van Gogh: Genius and Disaster* (New York: Harry N. Abrams, 1985)

E Ong

William J. Havlicek, *Van Gogh's Untold Journey* (Amsterdam: Creative Storytellers, 2010)

Robert Hughes, *Nothing If Not Critical* (The Harvill Press, 1990)

Jan Hulsker, *Vincent and Theo van Gogh: A dual biography* (Fuller Publications, Ann Arbor, 1990)

Jan Hulsker, *The Complete Van Gogh* (Oxford: Phaidon, 1980)

Robert Hughes, *Introduction. The Portable Van Gogh* (New York: Universe, 2002)

Albert J. Lubin, *Stranger on the earth: A psychological biography of Vincent van Gogh* (New York: Holt, Rinehart and Winston, 1972)

Melissa McQuillan, *Van Gogh* (London: Thames and Hudson, 1989)

Steven Naifeh and Gregory White Smith, *Van Gogh: the Life* (New York: Random House, 2011)

Arnold Pomerans, *The Letters of Vincent van Gogh* (London: Penguin Classics, 1997)

David Sweetman, *Van Gogh: His Life and His Art* (New York: Touchstone, 1990)

Marc Edo Tralbaut, *Vincent van Gogh, le mal aime* (Lausanne & MacMillam, London 1974)

Kenneth Wilkie, *The Van Gogh File: The Myth and the Man* (Souvenir Press Ltd, 2004)

David Smith, "Harry Potter and the man who conjured up Rowling's millions," (Guardian.co.uk, *The Observer*, July 15, 2007)

Potter tops 400 million sales, by Alison Flood (theBookseller.com 17 June 2008)

Marc Shapiro, *J.K. Rowling: The Wizard Behind Harry Potter* (St. Martin's Press, New York, 2000)

"Sunday Times Rich List—Joanne Rowling: Women's Rich List—Joanne Rowling" (*The Sunday Times*, April 27, 2008)

"No. 48 J.K. Rowling" (*Forbes Magazine,* June 14 2007)

Damien Pearse , "Harry Potter creator JK Rowling named Most Influential Woman in the UK" (*Guardian*, UK, October 11, 2010)

Decca Aitkenhead, "JK Rowling: The worst that can happen is that everyone says, That's shockingly bad (*The Guardian*, 2012)

Stephen McGinty, "The JK Rowling Story" (*The Scotsman,* June 16, 2003)

Collen A. Sexton, *J.K. Rowling* (Twenty-First Century Books, Brookfield, Connecticut, 2008)

"Person of the Year 2007 Runners-Up: J.K. Rowling" (*Time Magazine*, December 23, 2007)

"Happy birthday J.K. Rowling—Here are 10 magical facts about Harry Potter author" (*Los Angeles Times*, July 31, 2010)

Connie Ann Kirk, *J.K. Rowling: a biography* (Greenwood Press, Westport Connecticut, 2003)

"JK Rowling awarded honorary degree" (*Daily Telegraph,* July 8, 2004)

Melissa Anelli, *Harry, A History: The True Story of a Boy Wizard, His Fans, and Life Inside the Harry Potter Phenomenon* (New: Pocket)

Elisabeth Dunn, "From the dole to Hollywood" (*Daily Telegraph*, London), June 30, 2007)

Damien Henderson, "How JK Rowling has us spellbound" (*The Herald,* 2007)

Sean Smith, *J.K. Rowling: A Biography* (Michael O'Mara, London, 2003)

John Lawless, "Revealed: The eight-year-old girl who saved Harry Potter" (*The New Zealand Herald*, July 3, 2005)

Nigel Reynolds, "$100,000 Success Story for Penniless Mother" (*The Daily Telegraph*, July 7, 1997)

Lev Grossman, "J.K. Rowling Hogwarts And All" (*Time Magazine,* July 17, 2005)

"New Potter book topples U.S. sales records" (MSNBC, July 18, 2005)

"Harry Potter finale sales hit 11m" (BBC News, July 23, 2007)

"Rowling to kill two in final book" (London BBC News, June 27, 2006)

"Tears as JK Rowling returns to where it began" (*The Daily Telegraph,* December 24, 2007)

Jenny Sawyer, "Missing from Harry Potter—a real moral struggle" (*The Christian Science Monitor*, July 25, 2007)

"Final Harry Potter is expected to set record" (*The Boston Globe*, June 29, 2007)

Julie Watson and Tomas Kellner, "J.K. Rowling and the Billion-Dollar Empire" (Forbes.com, February 26, 2004)

Chapter 4: Lucky Break

Lord Patrick Kinross, *The Ottoman Centuries, The Rise and Fall of the Turkish Empire* (Perennial, HarperCollins Publishers Inc., 2002)

E Ong

Daniel Pipes, *Slave Soldiers and Islam—The Genesis of a Military System* (Yale University Press)

Godfrey Goodwin, *The Janissaries* (Saqi Books, 2001)

Jason Goodwin, *Lords of the Horizons: A History of the Ottoman Empire* (H. Holt, New York, 1998)

Barbara Jelavich, *History of the Balkans, 18th and 19th Centuries* (Cambridge University Press, 1983)

David Nicolle, *The Janissaries* (Osprey Publishing, London, 1995)

Radovan Samarcic, *Sokollu Mehmet Pasa* (Aralik, Istanbul, 2004)

Stephen R Turnbull, *The Ottoman Empire, 1326-1699* (Osprey Publishing Ltd, New York, 2003)

James Reston Jr., *Defenders of the Faith: Charles V, Suleyman the Magnificient, and the Battle for Europe, 1520-1536* (Marshall Cavendish, 2009)

Andrew Wheatcroft, The Enemy at the Gate: Habsuburgs, Ottomans, and the Battle for Europe (Basic Books, 2009)

J. Freely, *Istanbul: The Imperial City* (Penguin, 1998)

Stanford J. Shaw, History of the Ottoman Empire and Modern Turkey (Cambridge University Press, 1976)

Leslie P. Pierce, *The Imperial Harem, Women and Sovereignty in the Ottoman Empire* (Oxford University Press, 1993)

Thomas M. Prymak, "Roxolana: Wife of Suleiman the Magnificent" (*Nashe zhyttia/Our Life*, LII, 10, New York, 1995)

Galina Yermolenko, "Roxolana: The Greatest Empress of the East" (*The Muslim World*, 95, 2, 2005)

Chapter 5: To Survive Is to Succeed

Elli Wohlgelernter, "One Day That Shook The World" (*The Jerusalem Post*, April 30, 1998)

Steven Silbiger, *The Jewish Phenomenon—Seven Keys to the Enduring Wealth of a People* (Longstreet Press Inc., 2000)

"The World's 50 Richest Jews: 41-50," *The Jerusalem Post* (Israel), July 9, 2010

"The World's Billionaires: Frank Lowy," *Forbes*

E Ong

"Frank Lowy: From Hagana to $3.8 billion magnate," *The Jerusalem Post*

Jennifer Hewitt, "Holocaust truth set Frank Lowy free" (*The Australian*, November 3, 2010)

Forbes Billionaires March 2012: Joseph Safra

"The Safra Dynasty: The Mysterious Family of the Richest Banker in the World" (www.businessinsider.com)

Simon Romero, "International Business: The Safras of Brazil: Banking, Faith and Security" (*New York Times*, December 8, 1999)

Howard M. Sachar, *A History of the Jews in the Modern World* (Vintage Books, New York, 2005)

Sassoon, *Jewish Encyclopedia* 1906

Indian Jews, *Jewish Encyclopedia* 1906

Beverly Sasson, Vidal Sasson: A Year of Beauty and Health (Simon & Schuster, New York, 1975)

Sorry I Kept You Waiting, Madam—Autobiography of Vidal Sassoon (1968)

Vidal Sassoon, Vidal: The Autobiography (Macmillan, London, 2010)

"Turkey Needs a Mentality Revolution—Interview with Ishak Alaton," Qantara.de

"Citation of Public Orator, Dr Elaine Yee-lin Ho for the Honorary Michael David Kadoorie—169th Congregation" website of The University of Hong Kong, 2004

Jane S. Gerber, *The Jews of Spain—A history of the Sephardic Experience* (The Free Press, New York, 1994)

Kevin Alan Brook, The Jews of Khazaria (Jason Aronson Inc., New Jersey, 1999)

Ken Blady, *Jewish Communities in Exotic Places* (Jason Aronson Inc., New Jersey, 2000)

Esther Benbassa and Aron Rodrigue, *Sephardi Jewry, A History of the Judeo-Spanish Community, 14th-20th Centuries* (University of California Press, 2006)

Paul Kriwaczek, *Yiddish Civilisation, The Rise and Fall of a Forgotten Nation* (Vintage Books, New York 2006)

Gerard Chaliand and Jean-Pierre Rageau, *The Penguin Atlas of Diasporas* (Penguin Group, 1995)

Robert Bartlett, *The Making of Europe, Conquests, Colonization and Cultural Change 950-1350* (Penguin Group, 1994)

E Ong

Herbert A. Davidson, Moses Maimonides: The Man and his Works (OUP, 2005)

Abraham Joshua Heschel, *Maimonides: The Life and Times of a Medieval Jewish Thinker* (Farrar Strauss, New York, 1982)

Chapter 6: The Chinese Phenomenon

Geoff Hiscock, *Asia's New Wealth Club* (Nicholas Brealey Publishing 2000)

Thomas Sowell, *Migrations and Cultures—A World View* (Basic Books, a member of Perseus Books Group, 1996)

Jonathan D. Spence, *God's Chinese Son, The Taiping Heavenly Kingdom of Hong Xiuquan* (W.W. Norton & Company Inc., New York & London, 1996)

Lynn Pan, *Sons of the Yellow Emperor—The Story of the Overseas Chinese* (Arrow Books, 1998)

Lynn Pan (general editor), *The Encyclopedia of the Chinese Overseas* (Editions Didier Millet, published for Chinese Heritage Centre, 2006)

Thomas J. Stanley and William D. Danko, *The Millionaire Next Door* (Pocket Books, A division of Simon & Schuster Inc., New York, 1998)

Steven Silbiger, *The Jewish Phenomenon—Seven Keys to the Enduring Wealth of a People* (Longstreet Press Inc., 2000)

Chapter 7: Parable of the Seed

"A Decade of Dominance for McKinsey & Company in Vault Consulting Prestige Rankings," *Vault*, August 25, 2011

David Leonhardt, "Consultant Nation" (*The New York Times*, December 10, 2011)

"McKinsey & Company on Forbes' America's Largest Private Companies List," *Forbes*, November 3, 2010

John Huey, "How McKinsey Does It" by (*Fortune*, November 1, 1993)

James Kin, "McKinsey: CEO Factory, USA" (*USA Today*, May 19, 1993)

John A Byrne, "The McKinsey Mystique" (*BusinessWeek*, September 19, 1993)

Grayden Webb, *The History of the University of Cambridge and Education in England* (Cambridge University Press, 2005)

Christopher Brooke and Roger Highfield, *Oxford and Cambridge* (Cambridge University Press, 1988)

　　　　　　　　　　E Ong

Jeremy Catto, *The History of the University of Oxford* (Oxford Press, 1994)

Negley Harte and John North, *The World of UCL 1828-2004* (UCL, London, 2004)

Polly Curtis, "Poorer students get raw deal at work" (*The Guardian,* February 19, 2004)

James Melkle, "Third of Oxbridge comes from 100 schools" (Guardian.co.uk, September 20, 2007)

"Sutton Trust Report—University admissions by individual schools," September 2007

Lee Elliot Major, "This simplistic solution to Oxbridge elitism won't work" (Guardian.co.uk, May 28, 2010)

"UK/Education/State school participation rate" (BBC News, June 4, 2009)

Graeme Paton, "'Rich thick kids' do better at school, says Gove" (Telegraph.co.uk, July 28, 2010)

Jeevan Vasagar, "Fears for state pupils as top universities insist on A* at A-Level" (Guardian.co.uk, August 2, 2010)

Epilogue

Nicholas D Kristoff, "Kokura, Japan: Bypassed by A-Bomb" (*The New York Times,* August 7, 1995)

Tale of Two Cities: Hiroshima and Nagasaki (www.atomicarchive.com)

Paul Jenkins (director), Arturo Mio, Subreal Productions (producer), *Kanji Ishiwara, The Man Who Triggered the War* (Documentary, 2012)

Timothy P. Maga, *Judgment at Tokyo: The Japanese War Crimes Trials* (University Press of Kentucky, 2001)

Mark R. Peattie, *Ishiwara Kanji and Japan's confrontation with the West* (NJ: Princeton University Press, 1975)

Richard J. Samuels, *Securing Japan: Tokyo's Grand Strategy and the Future of East Asia* (Cornell University Press, 2007)

Daniel Moran, *Wars of National Liberation* (Cassell & Co, 2001)

Jung Chang and Jon Halliday, *Mao: The Unknown Story* (Alfred A. Knopf, 2005)

Ed Jocelyn and Andrew McEwen, *The Long March* (Constable and Robinson, 2006)

Harrison Evans Salisbury, *The Long March: The Untold Story* (Harper & Row, New York, 1985)

E Ong

E Ong